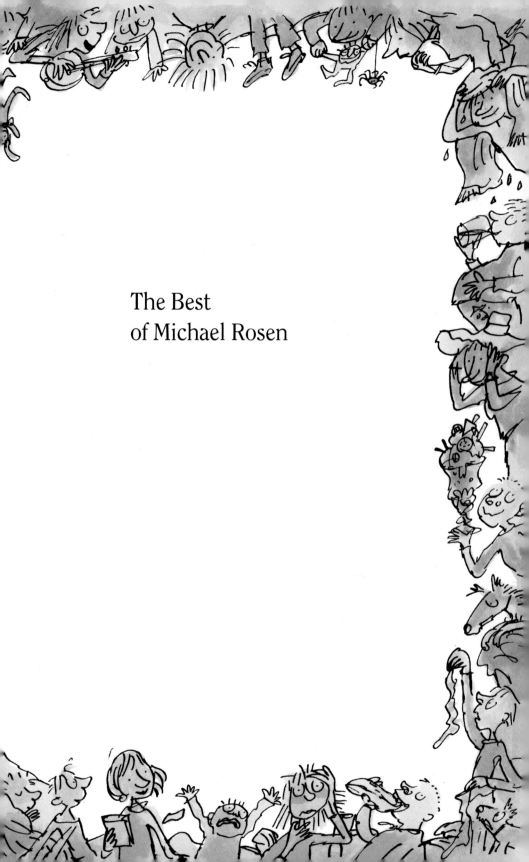

The Best
of Michael Rosen

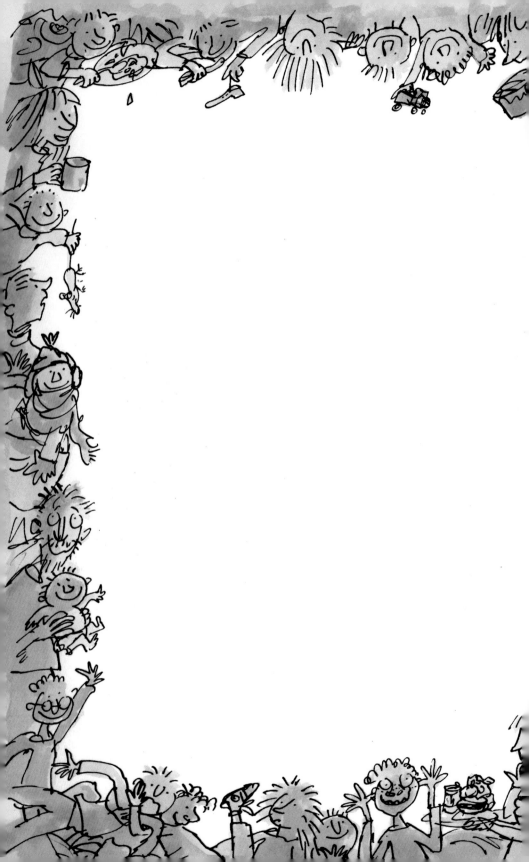

The Best
of Michael Rosen

Illustrated by
Quentin Blake

Introduction by
Ken and Yetta Goodman

Wetlands Press
A division of RDR Books

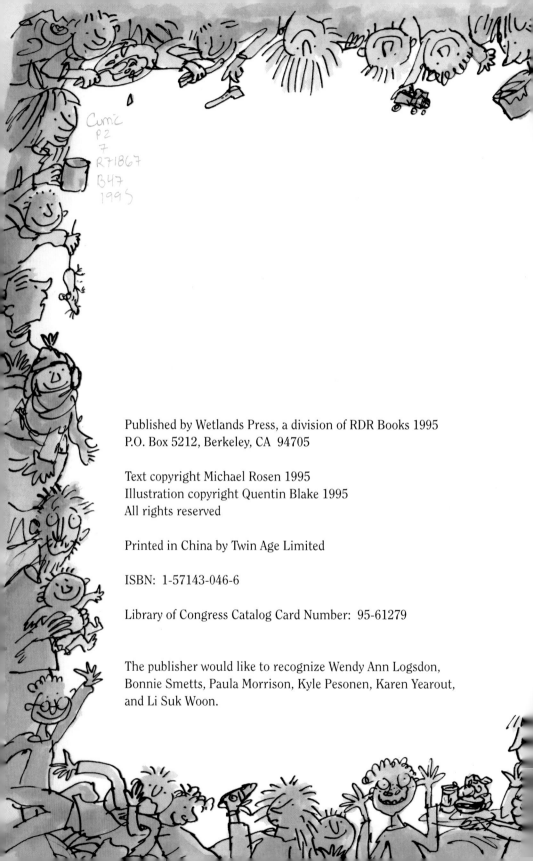

Published by Wetlands Press, a division of RDR Books 1995
P.O. Box 5212, Berkeley, CA 94705

Printed in China by Twin Age Limited

ISBN: 1-57143-046-6

Library of Congress Catalog Card Number: 95-61279

The publisher would like to recognize Wendy Ann Logsdon,
Bonnie Smetts, Paula Morrison, Kyle Pesonen, Karen Yearout,
and Li Suk Woon.

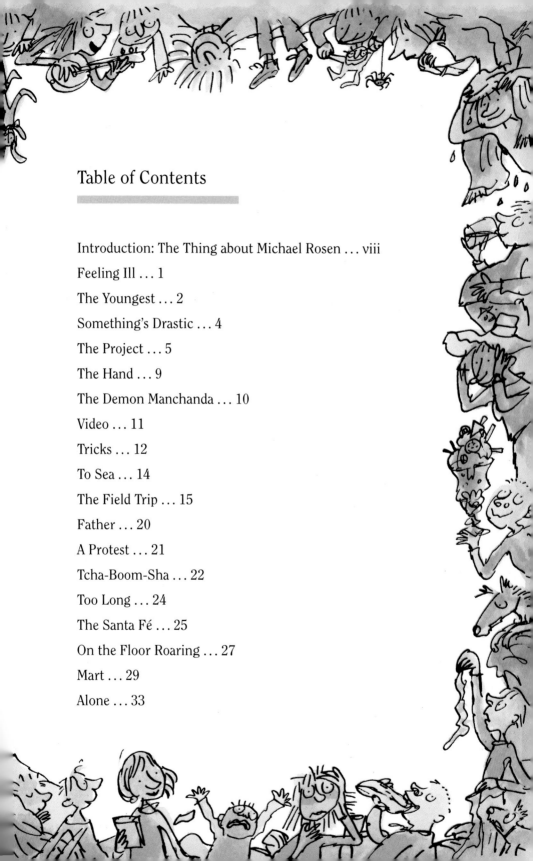

Table of Contents

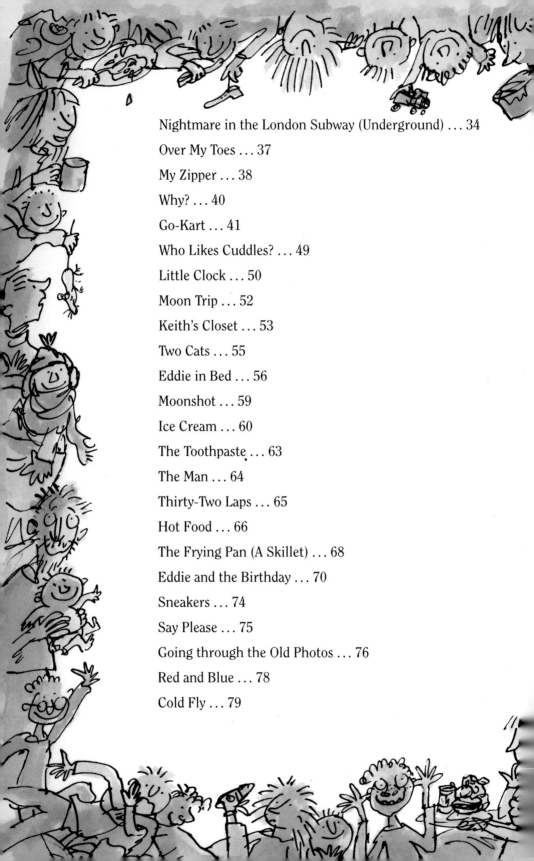

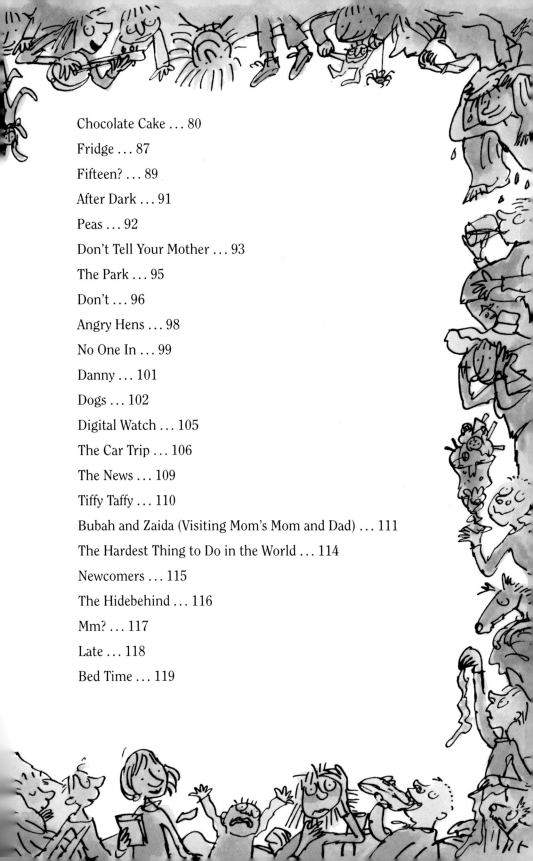

The Thing about Michael Rosen

The thing about Michael Rosen —
you can see it in his face. You just take one look at Michael Rosen —
even in a photo — and you can see it.
The thing about Michael Rosen
is he can turn himself back into the kid he was before he grew up.
You can see by the way he can scrunch up his face
and make you laugh just looking at him
before he even says anything.
It's not a grown-up face that stays the same most of the time.
It's a kid's face and behind it is a kid's way of seeing the world.
Michael Rosen can make his head — inside and out—
go back to being four years old or six or ten or twelve.
But then a funny thing happens:
when he tells about something in his six year old head,
or in his twelve year old head, it comes out a poem.
His nightmare about being between the lines
with the train coming in the London Underground — subway to us —
is just the way he dreamt it
but it has the clickety clack rhythm of the subway train.

And when he's ten or so
and pulls himself out of the pool
after swimming a whole mile
and a big man tells him that another lad — kid to us —
can swim ninety laps which is almost three miles
that comes out a poem too. And we know just how he felt
'cause the poem ends like a balloon that's just been popped.

So now you understand why Michael Rosen is the favorite poet of kids in England. And why grown-ups like him too. And you may also understand why you don't have to be Jewish or British to feel like he did in his poem about the pleasure of sharing a secret supper in his Jewish British home with his father and his brother on the night his mom had gone to class. He got to eat *matzo bray* — and even if you have no idea what that is — you know it tasted wonderful just because his mom would think it wasn't good for him.

When you've laughed over what Michael does with words you may not be surprised that his mom and dad (Harold and Connie) wrote a book about children's language development: all they had to do was study Michael.

So the thing about Michael Rosen
is sometimes his poems are simple and silly
and you say I could have written one like that.
And so you do.
And then when you finish reading his poems
you say more poems please.
But there aren't any more
so you have to read them again
and write some more of your own.
That's the thing about Michael Rosen.

— Ken and Yetta Goodman

Welcome to American readers, Michael Rosen.

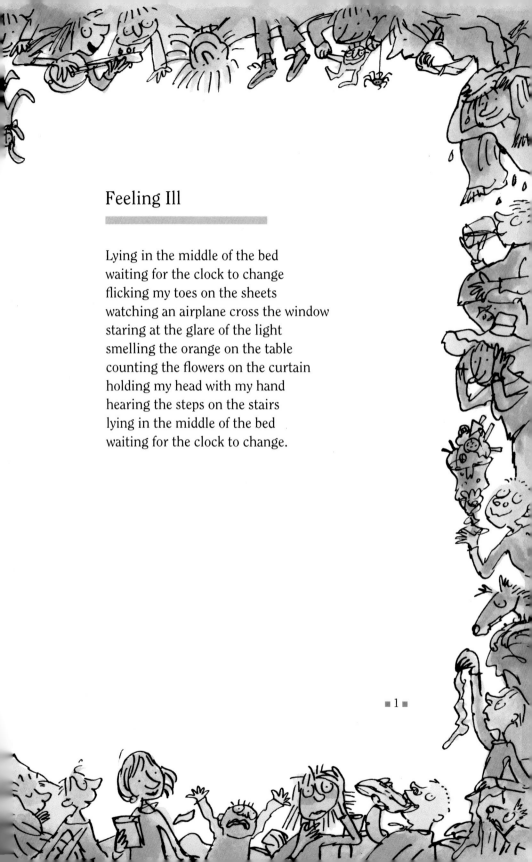

Feeling Ill

Lying in the middle of the bed
waiting for the clock to change
flicking my toes on the sheets
watching an airplane cross the window
staring at the glare of the light
smelling the orange on the table
counting the flowers on the curtain
holding my head with my hand
hearing the steps on the stairs
lying in the middle of the bed
waiting for the clock to change.

The Youngest

I'm the youngest in our house
so it goes like this:

My brother comes in and says:
"Tell him to clear the stuff
 out from under his bed."
 Mom says,
"Clear the stuff
 out from under your bed."
 Father says,
"You heard what your mother said."
"What?" I say.
"The stuff," he says.
"Clear the stuff
 out from under your bed."
 So I say,
"There's stuff under his bed, too,
 you know."
 So Father says,
"But we're talking about the stuff
 under *your* bed."
"You will clear it up
 won't you" Mom says.
 So now my brother — all puffed up —
 says,

"Clear the stuff
   out from under your bed,
   clear the stuff
   out from under your bed."
   Now I'm angry. I am angry.
   So I say — what shall I say?
   I say,
"Shuttup Stinks
   YOU CAN'T RULE MY LIFE."

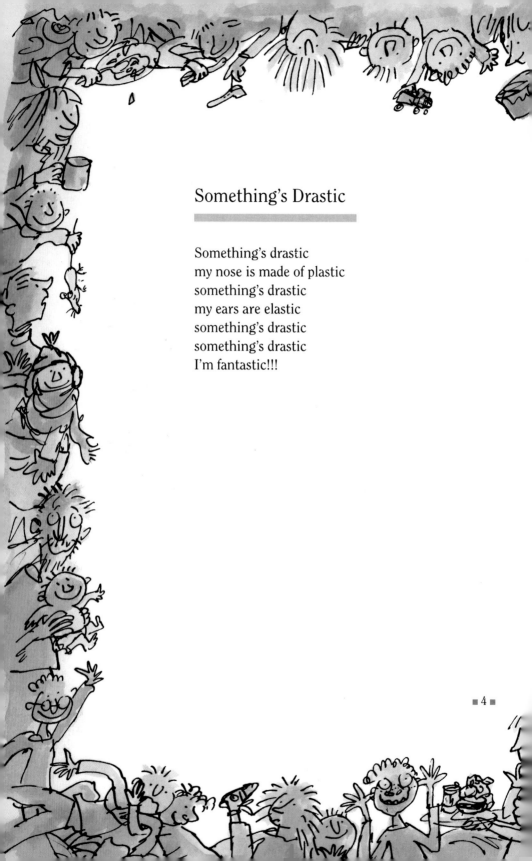

Something's Drastic

Something's drastic
my nose is made of plastic
something's drastic
my ears are elastic
something's drastic
something's drastic
I'm fantastic!!!

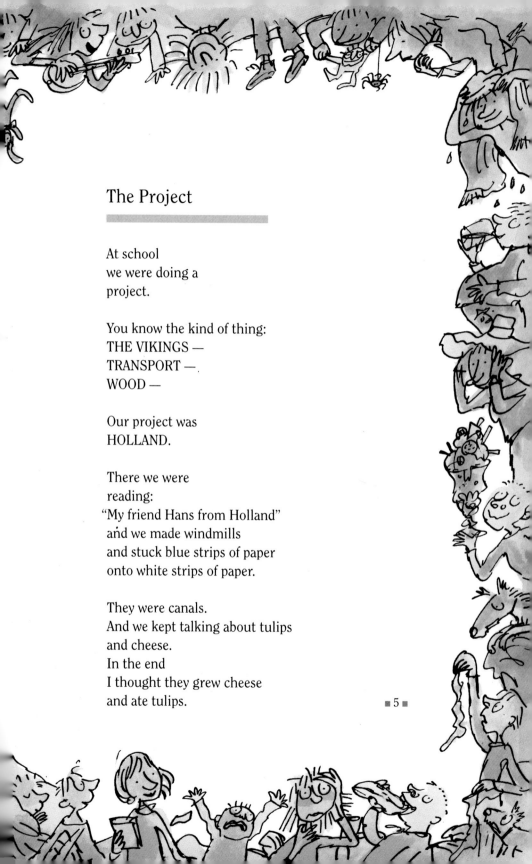

The Project

At school
we were doing a
project.

You know the kind of thing:
THE VIKINGS —
TRANSPORT —
WOOD —

Our project was
HOLLAND.

There we were
reading:
"My friend Hans from Holland"
and we made windmills
and stuck blue strips of paper
onto white strips of paper.

They were canals.
And we kept talking about tulips
and cheese.
In the end
I thought they grew cheese
and ate tulips.

Then suddenly one day
our teacher Miss Goodall
said that there was an inspector coming in.
She said he wasn't going to inspect us.
He was going to inspect her
and we were all to help her
by being really good
and answering all the questions that he asked us.

Later that day he came in.
He had a mustache.
We behaved.
Miss Goodall behaved.
There we all were sitting in our rows
behind our desks
breathing very very quietly
and he looked at our windmills
and our canals
and he said:
What do they eat in Holland?
And I didn't put my hand up
in case I said tulips
but Sheena Maclean said cheese
and he said:
What do they grow in Holland?
And I didn't put my hand up for that one
    either
but Margot Vane said tulips.
And he asked some more questions
and we were doing really well.
Miss Goodall was trying very hard

not to look proud
and then he asked:
Who is the queen of Holland?

There was silence.

No one knew who was the queen of Holland.

Miss Goodall frowned
and started looking all around the class
with her eyes looking all hoping.

Then suddenly I remembered this funny
    little rhyme
that my friend Harrybo used to say.

I put up my hand.

Yes, said the inspector.

Queen Juliana
is a fat banana,
I said.

Miss Goodall looked awful.
Harrybo was sitting in front of me
and I saw him snort and start giggling.

What did you say? asked the inspector.
Queen Juliana, I said.
Good, he said.

You're right, quite right.
Miss Goodall was delighted.
I was delighted.
The inspector was delighted.
And Harrybo was still snorting away like mad.

The Hand

This is the hand
that touched the frost
that froze my tongue
and made it numb.

This is the hand
that cracked the nut
that went in my mouth
and never came out.

This is the hand
that slid around the bath
to find the soap
that wouldn't float.

This is the hand
on the hot water bottle
meant to warm my bed
but got lost instead.

This is the hand
that held the bottle
that let go of the soap
that cracked the nut
that touched the frost.
This is the hand
that never gets lost.

The Demon Manchanda

The two-headed two-body,
the Demon Manchanda
had eyes bigger than his belly.
He walked and talked
right round the world
but every time he opened his mouth
he put his foot in it.

"You're pulling my leg,"
he said to himself.
So he ate his words instead.
I guess you know the rest:
he went to the window
and threw out his chest.

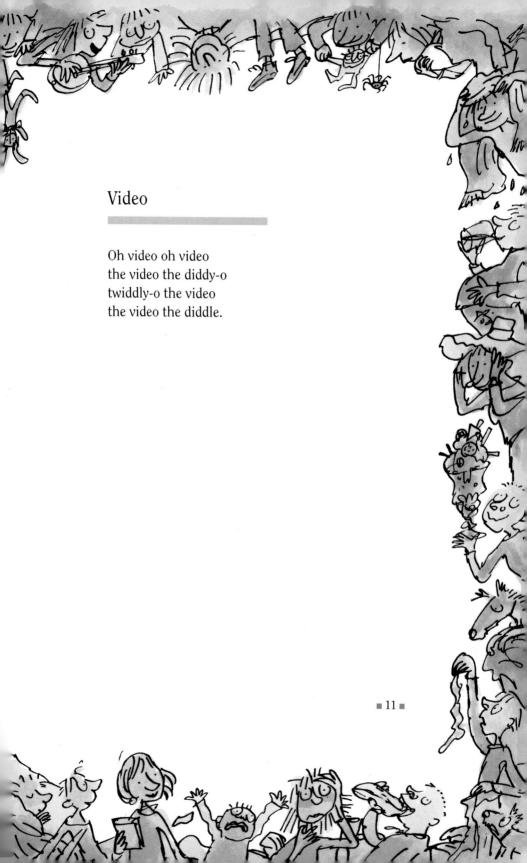

Video

Oh video oh video
the video the diddy-o
twiddly-o the video
the video the diddle.

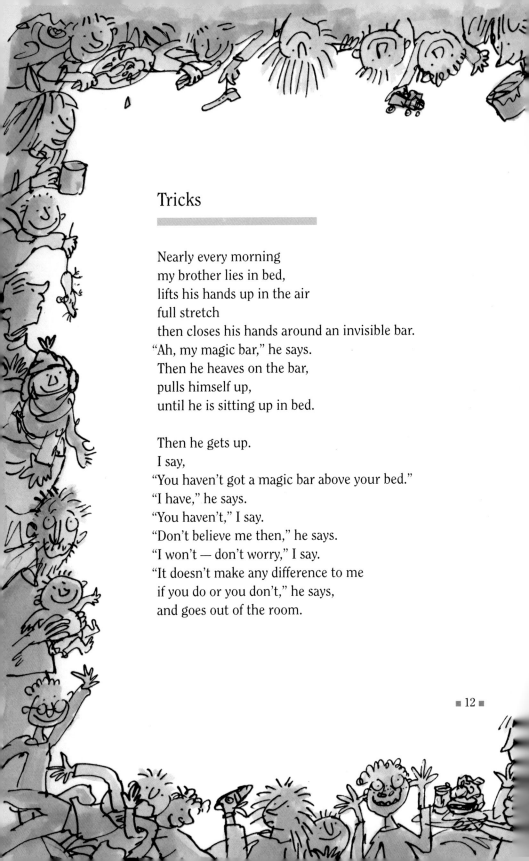

Tricks

Nearly every morning
my brother lies in bed,
lifts his hands up in the air
full stretch
then closes his hands around an invisible bar.
"Ah, my magic bar," he says.
Then he heaves on the bar,
pulls himself up,
until he is sitting up in bed.

Then he gets up.
I say,
"You haven't got a magic bar above your bed."
"I have," he says.
"You haven't," I say.
"Don't believe me then," he says.
"I won't — don't worry," I say.
"It doesn't make any difference to me
if you do or you don't," he says,
and goes out of the room.

"Magic bar!" I say.
"Crazy. He hasn't got a magic bar."
I make sure he's gone downstairs,
then I walk over to his bed
and wave my hand about in the air
above his pillow.
"I knew it," I say to myself.
"Didn't fool me for a moment."

To Sea

I put out to sea
in a wooden rowboat
with a cheese and pickle sandwich
and a yellow hat and coat.

The Field Trip

All right, class six
ALL RIGHT, CLASS SIX
I'm talking

I'm talking
I want complete quiet
and that includes you, David Alexander,
yes, you
no need to turn around, David
there aren't any other David Alexanders here, are there?
Louise
it isn't absolutely necessary for your watch
to play London's Burning just now, is it?

All right
as you know
it was our plan to go out today —
to the Science Museum.
Now I had hoped that it would not be necessary
for me to have to tell you —
yes, you as well, Abdul,
you're in class six as well, aren't you?
I saw that, Mark,
I saw it.
Any more and you'll be out.
No trip,
nothing.

I had hoped that it wouldn't be necessary
for me to tell you how to BEHAVE
when we go on a trip.

But —
and this is a big but —
you haven't heard a word I've said, have you, Donna?
This is a big but
I HAVE to tell you how to behave, don't I?
Why?

Yes, it IS because you never listen
but there's another reason, isn't there?
Yes, Warren,
because of what happened last time.

Let us remind ourselves of a few things:
The food —
Even as I speak
would you believe it?
I can see that Phanh has opened her can of soda
I do not believe it
I really don't.
Do we have lunch at nine-thirty at school?
No,
we have lunch at twelve-fifteen
but, Phanh, you've already begun yours.
If you remember,
last time
Joanna had eaten all her sandwiches
before she even got to school.

■ 16 ■

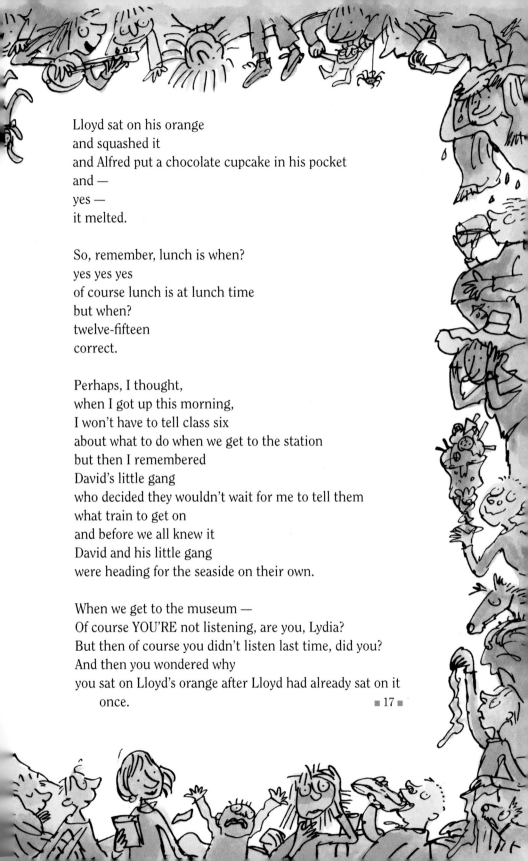

Lloyd sat on his orange
and squashed it
and Alfred put a chocolate cupcake in his pocket
and —
yes —
it melted.

So, remember, lunch is when?
yes yes yes
of course lunch is at lunch time
but when?
twelve-fifteen
correct.

Perhaps, I thought,
when I got up this morning,
I won't have to tell class six
about what to do when we get to the station
but then I remembered
David's little gang
who decided they wouldn't wait for me to tell them
what train to get on
and before we all knew it
David and his little gang
were heading for the seaside on their own.

When we get to the museum —
Of course YOU'RE not listening, are you, Lydia?
But then of course you didn't listen last time, did you?
And then you wondered why
you sat on Lloyd's orange after Lloyd had already sat on it
    once.

■ 17 ■

When we get to the museum
do we run about the halls?
Do we run around screaming?
Do we go sliding on the shiny floors?
No we don't
no we don't
no we don't.

Thank you, Mervyn, that's enough
I'm very glad you've got jam in your sandwiches,
    Mervyn,
we are all glad that you've got jam in your sandwiches,
    Mervyn,
but what has it got to do with sliding on the floor of the
    Science Museum?
Precisely nothing.
I'm very sorry, Mervyn, but nobody,
nobody at all
wants to know about the jam in your sandwiches,
    Mervyn.

Now,
when you're ready
when you're quiet
we'll all go.
That doesn't mean leaping up in the air, Karen,
does it?
Louise, why is your watch now playing
For He's A Jolly Good Fellow?
Yes, I know it could be SHE'S A Jolly Good Fellow, Zoe,
but that isn't what we are talking about, is it?

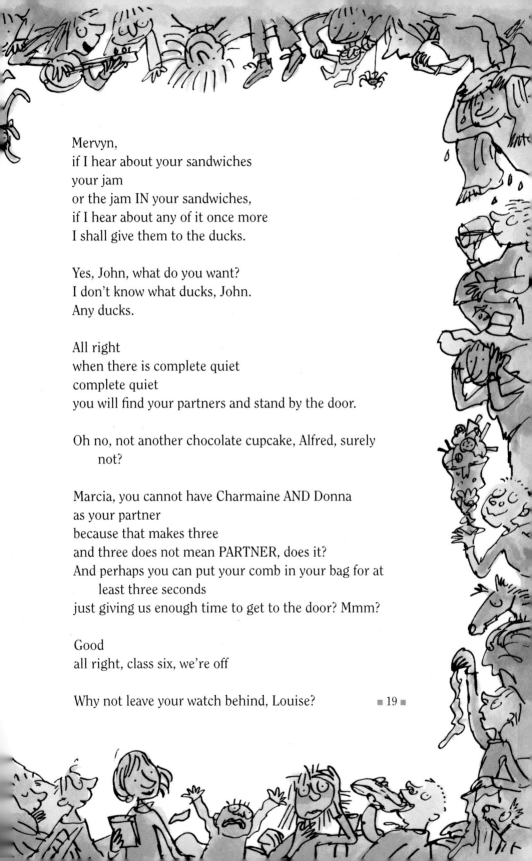

Mervyn,
if I hear about your sandwiches
your jam
or the jam IN your sandwiches,
if I hear about any of it once more
I shall give them to the ducks.

Yes, John, what do you want?
I don't know what ducks, John.
Any ducks.

All right
when there is complete quiet
complete quiet
you will find your partners and stand by the door.

Oh no, not another chocolate cupcake, Alfred, surely
    not?

Marcia, you cannot have Charmaine AND Donna
as your partner
because that makes three
and three does not mean PARTNER, does it?
And perhaps you can put your comb in your bag for at
    least three seconds
just giving us enough time to get to the door? Mmm?

Good
all right, class six, we're off

Why not leave your watch behind, Louise?

■ 19 ■

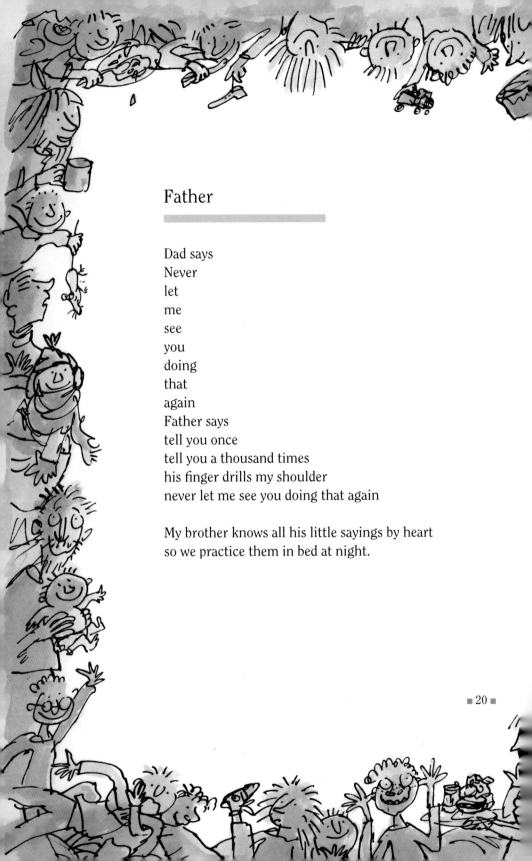

Father

Dad says
Never
let
me
see
you
doing
that
again
Father says
tell you once
tell you a thousand times
his finger drills my shoulder
never let me see you doing that again

My brother knows all his little sayings by heart
so we practice them in bed at night.

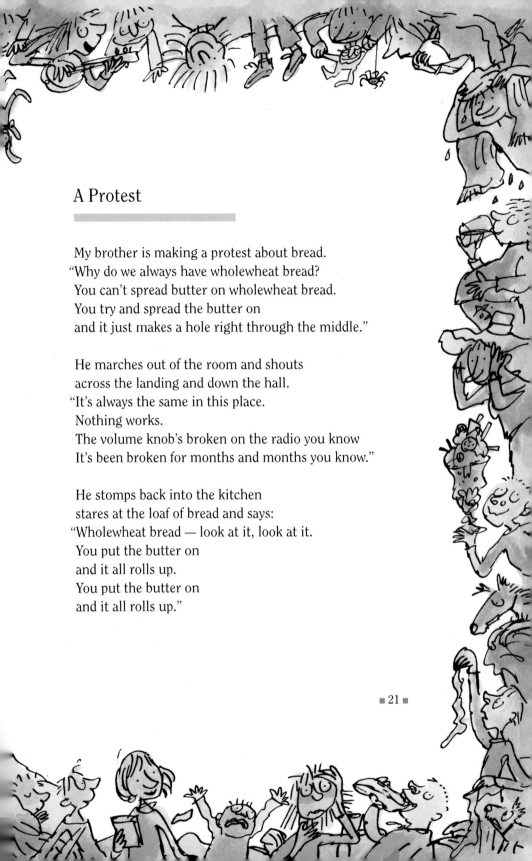

A Protest

My brother is making a protest about bread.
"Why do we always have wholewheat bread?
You can't spread butter on wholewheat bread.
You try and spread the butter on
and it just makes a hole right through the middle."

He marches out of the room and shouts
across the landing and down the hall.
"It's always the same in this place.
Nothing works.
The volume knob's broken on the radio you know
It's been broken for months and months you know."

He stomps back into the kitchen
stares at the loaf of bread and says:
"Wholewheat bread — look at it, look at it.
You put the butter on
and it all rolls up.
You put the butter on
and it all rolls up."

Tcha-Boom-Sha

I'm in my mom

on one hand
one thumb
on the other hand
another one

I'm in my mom

in the middle of me
I've got
tcha-boom-sha
tcha-boom-sha
tcha-boom-sha
a heart

in the middle of me
I hear
ca-boom
ca-boom
ca-boom
her heart

in here
we go
tcha-boom-sha
tcha-boom-sha
tcha-boom-sha
ca-boom
tcha-boom-sha
tcha-boom-sha
tcha-boom-sha
ca-boom

I'm in my mom

Too Long

Every few weeks someone looks at me and says:
my you've grown
and then every few weeks someone says:
they've grown too long

and silver scissors come out of the drawer
and chip at my toes and run through my hair

Now I don't like this one little bit.
I won't grow if I'm going to be chopped.
What's me is mine and I want to keep it
so either the scissors or my nails had better stop.

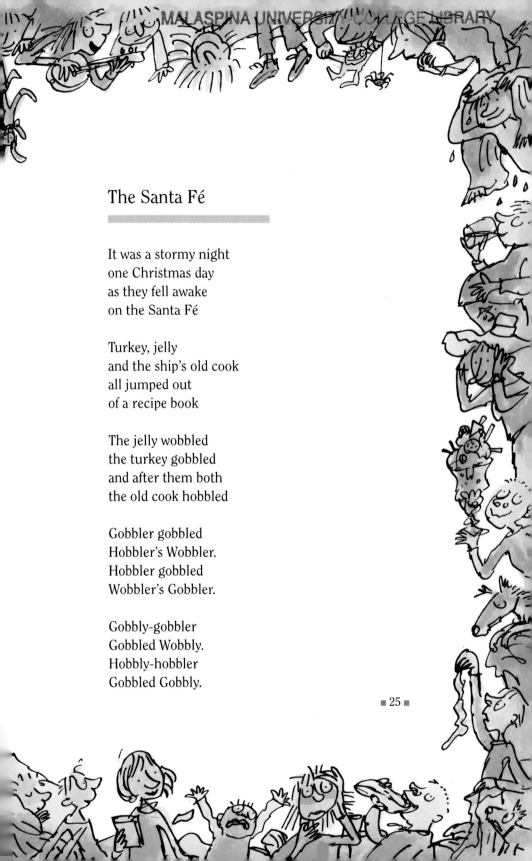

The Santa Fé

It was a stormy night
one Christmas day
as they fell awake
on the Santa Fé

Turkey, jelly
and the ship's old cook
all jumped out
of a recipe book

The jelly wobbled
the turkey gobbled
and after them both
the old cook hobbled

Gobbler gobbled
Hobbler's Wobbler.
Hobbler gobbled
Wobbler's Gobbler.

Gobbly-gobbler
Gobbled Wobbly.
Hobbly-hobbler
Gobbled Gobbly.

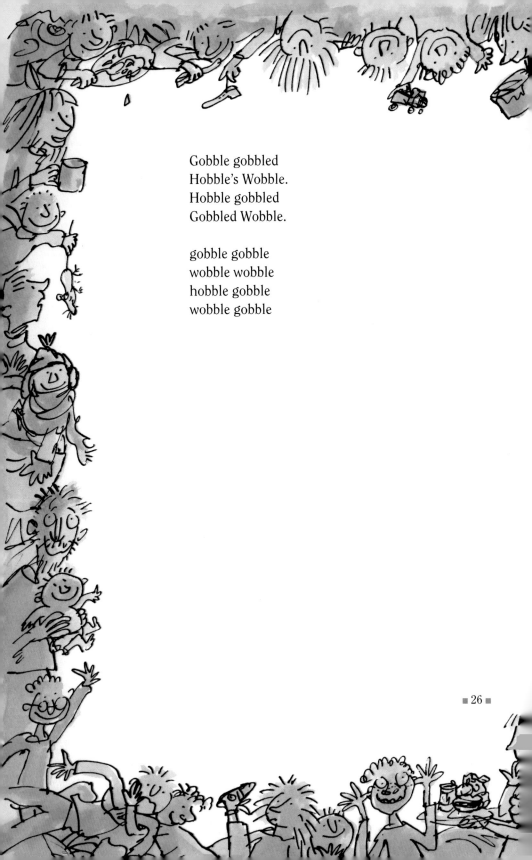

Gobble gobbled
Hobble's Wobble.
Hobble gobbled
Gobbled Wobble.

gobble gobble
wobble wobble
hobble gobble
wobble gobble

On the Floor Roaring

My brother's on the floor roaring
my brother's on the floor roaring
why is my brother on the floor roaring?
My brother is on the floor roaring
because he's supposed to finish his beans
before he has his pudding.

But he doesn't want to finish his beans
before he has his pudding

he says he wants his pudding
NOW.

But they won't let him

so now my brother is . . . on the floor roaring.

They're saying
I give you one more chance to finish those beans
or you don't go to Tony's
but he's not listening because . . .
he's on the floor roaring.

He's getting yelled at
I'm not
I've eaten my beans.

Do you know what I'm doing now?
I'm eating my pudding
and . . . he's on the floor roaring.

If he wasn't . . . on the floor roaring
he'd see me eating my pudding
and if he looked really close
he might see a little tiny smile
just at the corner of my mouth.
But he's not looking . . .
he's on the floor roaring.

The pudding is okay
it's not wonderful
not wonderful enough
to be sitting on the floor and roaring about
unless you're my brother.

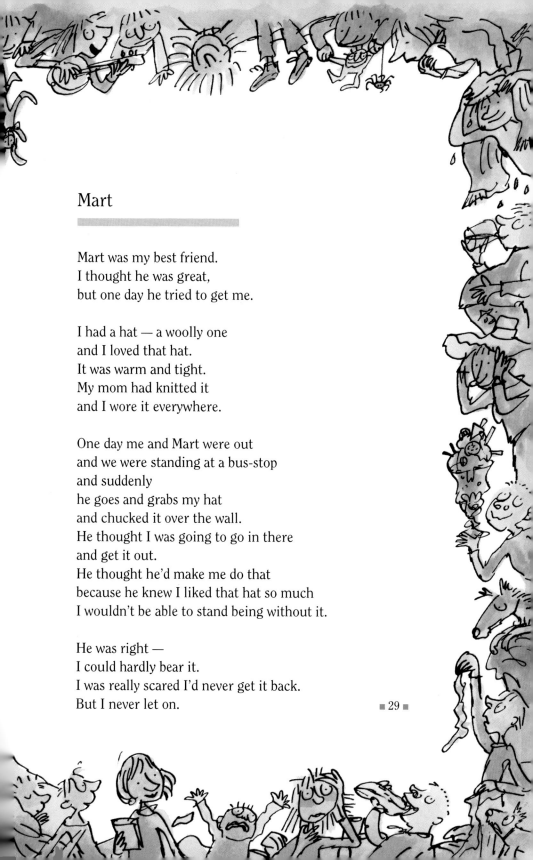

Mart

Mart was my best friend.
I thought he was great,
but one day he tried to get me.

I had a hat — a woolly one
and I loved that hat.
It was warm and tight.
My mom had knitted it
and I wore it everywhere.

One day me and Mart were out
and we were standing at a bus-stop
and suddenly
he goes and grabs my hat
and chucked it over the wall.
He thought I was going to go in there
and get it out.
He thought he'd make me do that
because he knew I liked that hat so much
I wouldn't be able to stand being without it.

He was right —
I could hardly bear it.
I was really scared I'd never get it back.
But I never let on.

I never showed it on my face.
I just waited.

"Aren't you going to get your hat?"
he says.
"Your hat's gone," he says.
"Your hat's over the wall."
I looked the other way.

But I could still feel on my head
how he had pulled it off.
"Your hat's over the wall," he says.
I didn't say a thing.

Then the bus came round the corner
at the end of the road.

If I go home without my hat
I'm going to walk through the door
and Mom's going to say,
"Where's your hat?"
and if I say,
"It's over the wall,"
she's going to say,
"What's it doing there?"
and I'm going to say,
"Mart chucked it over,"
and she's going to say,
"Why didn't you go for it?"
and what am I going to say then?
what am I going to say then?

The bus was coming up.
"Aren't you going over for your hat?
There won't be another bus for ages,"
Mart says.

The bus was coming closer.
"You've lost your hat now,"
Mart says.

The bus stopped.
I got on
Mart got on
The bus moved off.

"You've lost your hat," Mart says.

"You've lost your hat," Mart says.

Two stops ahead, was ours.
"Are you going indoors without it?" Mart says.
I didn't say a thing.

The bus stopped.

Mart got up
and dashed to the front.
He'd got off one stop early.
I got off when we got to our stop.

I went home
walked through the door

■ 31 ■

"Where's your hat?" Mom says.
"Over a wall," I said.
"What's it doing there?" she says.
"Mart chucked it over there," I said.
"But you haven't left it there, have you?" she says.
"Yes," I said.
"Well don't you ever come asking me to make you
  anything like that again.
  You make me tired, you do."

Later,
I was drinking some orange juice.
The front door-bell rang.
It was Mart.
He had the hat in his hand.
He handed it to me — and went.

I shut the front door —
put on the hat
and walked into the kitchen.
Mom looked up.

"You don't need to wear your hat indoors do you?"
  she said.
"I will for a bit," I said.
  And I did.

Alone

I'm alone in the evening
when the family sits
reading and sleeping
and I watch the fire up close
to see flame goblins
wriggling out of their caves
for the evening

Later I'm alone
when the bath has gone cold around me
and I have put my foot
beneath the cold tap
where it can dribble
through valleys between my toes
out across the white plain of my foot
and bibble bibble into the sea

I'm alone
when Mom's switched out the light
my head against the pillow
listening to ca thump ca thump
in the middle of my ears.
It's my heart.

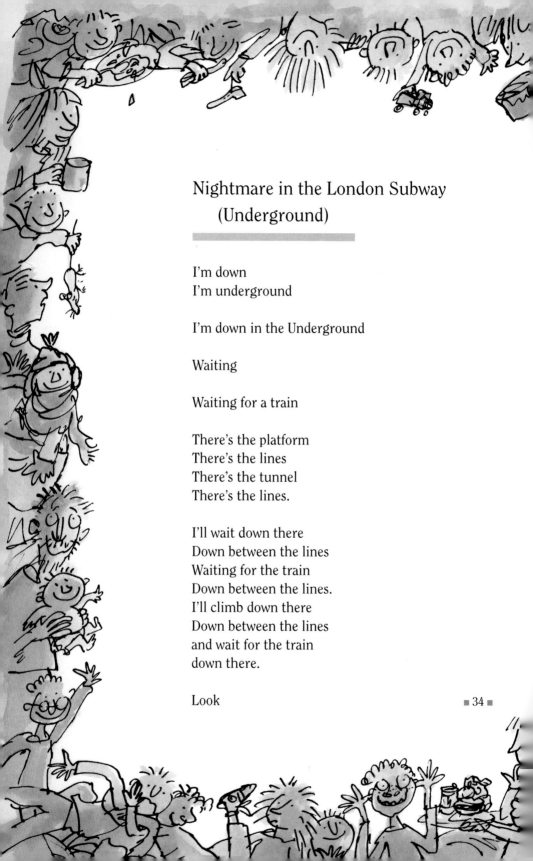

Nightmare in the London Subway
(Underground)

I'm down
I'm underground

I'm down in the Underground

Waiting

Waiting for a train

There's the platform
There's the lines
There's the tunnel
There's the lines.

I'll wait down there
Down between the lines
Waiting for the train
Down between the lines.
I'll climb down there
Down between the lines
and wait for the train
down there.

Look

Look up the tunnel look
Yes it's coming, it's coming
they say,

And it is.
And I'm between the lines.

And I can see it
See it coming
and I'm between the lines.

Can someone give me a
hand up?
Can't you see?

I'm between the lines
and the train's coming.
Can't you see?

I'm between the lines
and the train's coming.
Give me a hand someone
give me a hand
the train's coming
give me a hand
I can't climb up.
The train's coming
and the platform's sliding in
towards me too
with the train still coming
coming down the tunnel

the platform's sliding
sliding in towards me too.

I'm still down
Can't anyone see me
down between the lines?

Look
see
me
the train
platform
me
the train
near now
nearer now
nearer and nearer now
NOW

That's all.

Over My Toes

Over my toes
goes
the soft sea wash
see the sea wash
the soft sand slip
see the sea slip
the soft sand slide
see the sea slide
the soft sand slap
the soft sand wash
over my toes.

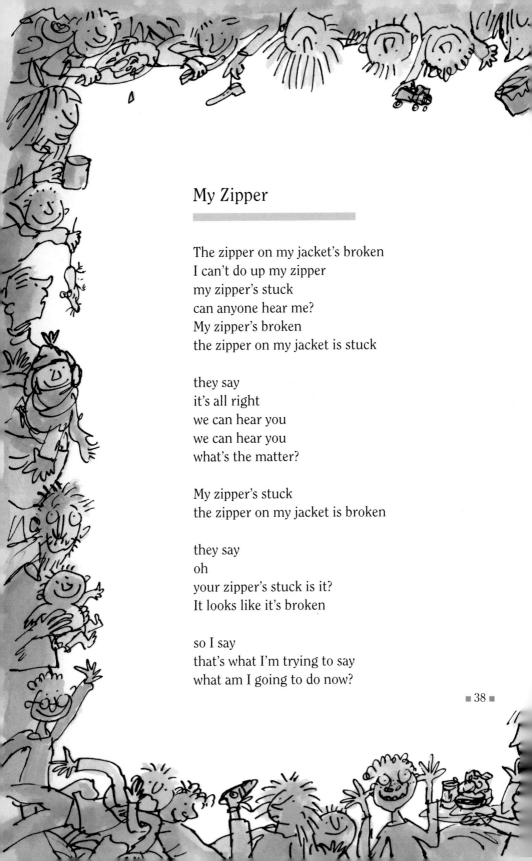

My Zipper

The zipper on my jacket's broken
I can't do up my zipper
my zipper's stuck
can anyone hear me?
My zipper's broken
the zipper on my jacket is stuck

they say
it's all right
we can hear you
we can hear you
what's the matter?

My zipper's stuck
the zipper on my jacket is broken

they say
oh
your zipper's stuck is it?
It looks like it's broken

so I say
that's what I'm trying to say
what am I going to do now?

They say,
well now
there's nothing much you can do with a broken zipper,
     you know
it's a shame but there you go, nothing lasts forever
what's done is done, one jacket down the drain, end of
     story

so I shout:
you're no good
you're all useless and horrible
all the time

and then I slam the door
very loudly.

They clapped.

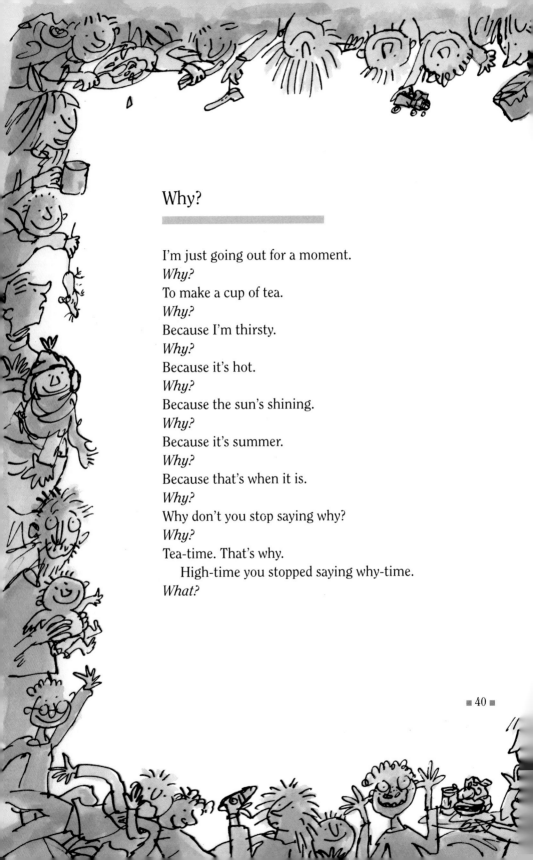

Why?

I'm just going out for a moment.
Why?
To make a cup of tea.
Why?
Because I'm thirsty.
Why?
Because it's hot.
Why?
Because the sun's shining.
Why?
Because it's summer.
Why?
Because that's when it is.
Why?
Why don't you stop saying why?
Why?
Tea-time. That's why.
    High-time you stopped saying why-time.
What?

Go-Kart

Me and my buddy Harrybo
we once made a go-kart.
Everyone was making go-karts
so we had to make one.
Big Tony's was terrific,
Big Tony was terrific
because Big Tony told us he was.
What he said was,
"I am TERRIFIC,"
And because Big Tony was VERY big
no one said,
"Big Tony.
You are NOT terrific."
So,
Big Tony was terrific,
and Big Tony's go-kart was terrific.
And that was that.

When Big Tony sat on his go-kart
he looked like a real driver.
He had control.
When he came down a road round our way
called Moss Lane
he could make the wind blow his hair,
pheeeeeeoooooooooph,

he could make the wheels of his go-kart go
prrrrrrrrrrrrrrrrrrr
and he went
eeeeeeeeeeeeeooowwwwwww
as he went past.
I was jealous of Big Tony.
I was afraid that I thought
he might be
terrific.

So me and Harrybo
we made a go-kart
out of his old stroller
and some boxes and crates
we got from the liquor store.
We nailed it up with bent nails
but Harrybo's dad said,
"No no no no no
you should use big metal staples,"
and he gave us some.
He said they were
Heavy Duty.

Heavy duty
wow
That sounded
terrific.

So then we tied rope around the front crosspiece.
But Harrybo's dad said,
"No no no no no,
you should use the stroller handle."

And he helped us fix
the stroller handle to the crosspiece.
He said, "That'll give you
Control."

Control
wow
That sounded
terrific.

Harrybo sat on the beer-crate
and steered,
I kneeled behind.
But Harrybo's dad said,
"No no no no no
you should kneel on foam pads."
And he cut these two foam pads
for me to kneel on.
Harrybo's dad said,
"That'll help you
Last The Course."

Last the course,
wow
That sounded
terrific.

Our go-kart was ready.

So we took it up to the top of Moss Lane
and Harrybo said,
"I'll steer," and he did.

It was fan
tastic.
It felt just like Big Tony looked.
The hair in the wind

pheeeeeeeoooooooooooph
the wheels
prrrrrrrrrrrrrrrrr
and so we both went
eeeeeeeeeeeeeoooowwwwwwwww

So we took it up to the top
of Moss Lane again
and Harrybo said,
"I'll steer,"
and he did.
It was a-
mazing.
The road went blurry.

The hair in the wind
pheeeeeeeooooooph
the wheels went
prrrrrrrrrrrrrr
so we both went
eeeeeeeeeoooowwwwwwwww

So we took it up to the top of Moss Lane again
and Harrybo said,
"I'll steer,"
so I said,
"Can I have a try?"

44

Harrybo said,
"NO."
"Come on," I said.
"No," he said, "You've never done it."
"Come on, Harrybo. Let me have a try.
Come on. I'll be your best friend.
Come on, Harrybo. Come on."
"No."
"Oh come on. Come on. Come on."

"All right," he said.
"Look out, won't you."
"Yeah yeah yeah. *I* know," I said.
I thought,
"I'm going to be
terrific."
My hair — pheeeoooph
wheels — prrrrrr
me — eeeow

And away we went
hair — yeah — pheeeeeeeeeooooph
wheels — yeah — prrrrrrrrrrrrr
me — yeah — eeeeeeeeoooooooow
BUT
halfway down Moss Lane
there's Moss Close
and that's where the road curves
and that's where Big Tony steers
Big Tony leans
Big Tony controls
prrrrrrrrrr

eeeeeeoooowwww
I saw Moss Close coming up really fast . . .
"Steer." Shouts Harrybo. "Steer, you big jerk!"
And I yanked on the stroller handle
ugh
and the whole world
went round once and twice
and three times
and my head went rolling
down the road
pulling me after it
and the go-kart came for the ride
over and over and over
until my nose and my chin
and my two front teeth landed up
in the grit of the gutter.
Harrybo was crying.
"Wo wo wo oooo wo wo ooo."
I breathed in and it whistled.
"Whew."
"Whew."
There it was again.
I stuck my finger up to my tooth
and it was chipped.
Harrybo said,
"Your chin's bleeding,"
and I said,
"Your chin's bleeding an' all."
"I know ooooooo," he said.

We walked home.
He pulled the kart,

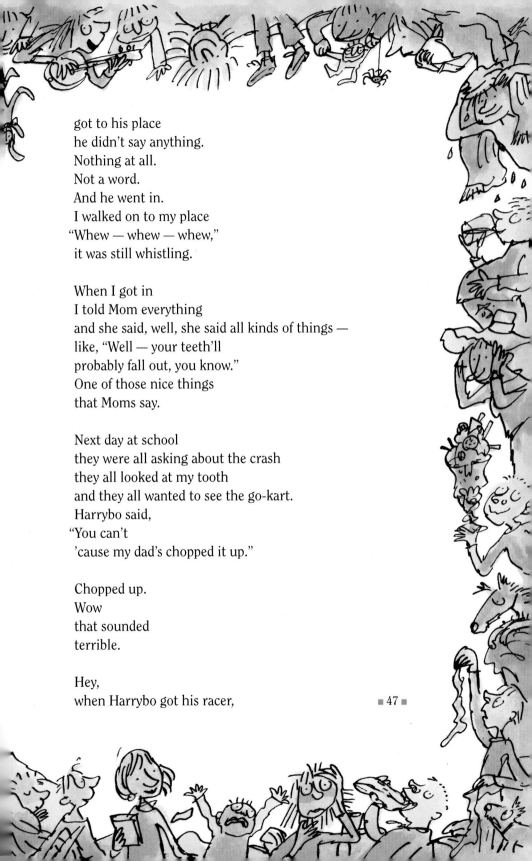

got to his place
he didn't say anything.
Nothing at all.
Not a word.
And he went in.
I walked on to my place
"Whew — whew — whew,"
it was still whistling.

When I got in
I told Mom everything
and she said, well, she said all kinds of things —
like, "Well — your teeth'll
probably fall out, you know."
One of those nice things
that Moms say.

Next day at school
they were all asking about the crash
they all looked at my tooth
and they all wanted to see the go-kart.
Harrybo said,
"You can't
'cause my dad's chopped it up."

Chopped up.
Wow
that sounded
terrible.

Hey,
when Harrybo got his racer,

his brand new racing bike for Christmas
I didn't ask him for a ride on it.
I didn't
no
I didn't

I wonder why.

Who Likes Cuddles?

Who likes cuddles?
Me.
Who likes hugs?
Me.
Who likes squeezes?
Me.
Who likes tickles?
Me.
Who likes getting their face stroked?
Me.
Who likes being lifted up high?
Me.
Who likes sitting on laps?
Me.
Who likes being whirled round and round?
Me.
But best of all I like
getting into bed and getting blowy blowy
down my neck behind my ear.
A big warm tickly blow
lovely.

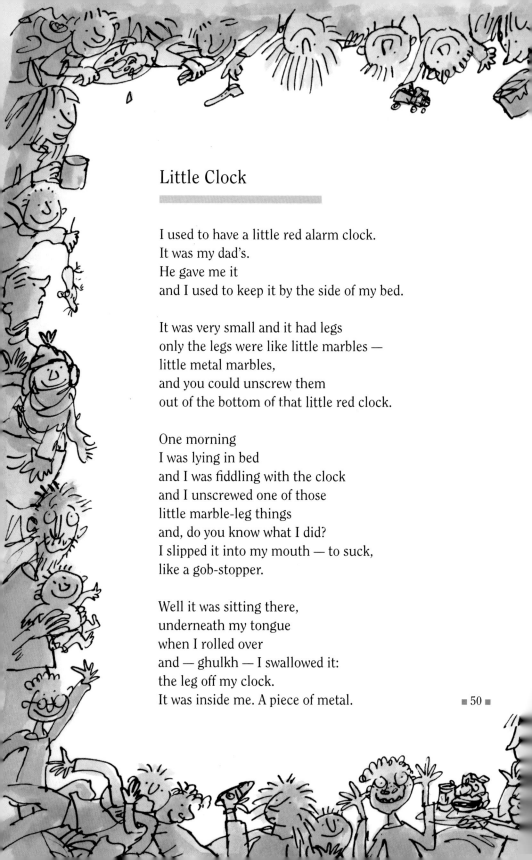

Little Clock

I used to have a little red alarm clock.
It was my dad's.
He gave me it
and I used to keep it by the side of my bed.

It was very small and it had legs
only the legs were like little marbles —
little metal marbles,
and you could unscrew them
out of the bottom of that little red clock.

One morning
I was lying in bed
and I was fiddling with the clock
and I unscrewed one of those
little marble-leg things
and, do you know what I did?
I slipped it into my mouth — to suck,
like a gob-stopper.

Well it was sitting there,
underneath my tongue
when I rolled over
and — ghulkh — I swallowed it:
the leg off my clock.
It was inside me. A piece of metal.

I looked at the clock.
It was leaning over on one side.
I stood it up and of course it fell over.

So I got up,
went downstairs with it
and I was holding it out in front of me
and I walked into the kitchen
and I said:
"Look, the clock. The leg. The leg. The clock — er . . ."

And my dad took it off me and he said,
"What's up, son? Did you lose it?
Not to worry, it can't have gone far.
We'll find it,
and we can screw it back on here, look."

"I swallowed it," I said.

"You swallowed it? You swallowed it?
Are you mad? Are you stark raving mad?
You've ruined a perfectly good clock.
That was a good clock, that was.
Now what's the use of a clock that won't stand up?"
He held it out in front of him,
and he stared at it. I looked at it too.
I was wondering what was happening to the leg.

Moon Trip

Humpty Dumpty went to the moon
on a supersonic spoon.
He took some porridge and a tent
but when he landed
the spoon got bent.
Humpty said,
"I don't care,"
and for all I know
he's still up there.

Keith's Closet

Have you looked in Keith's closet?
You ought to.
You've never seen anything like Keith's closet.
Let's go over to Keith's place
and look in Keith's closet.

So when you get to Keith's place
you say,
"Can we play in your garage?"
And he says,
"No."
So you say,
"Can we play in your tent?"
And he says,
"No."
So you say,
"Can we play with your crane?"
And he says,
"No."

So you go up to Keith's mom
and you say,
"Can we play in Keith's tent?"
And she says,

"Keith, Keith,
why don't you get the tent out?"
"Okay,"
says Keith,
and he starts going over to the closet —
Keith's closet.
He opens it, and —
Wow!

You've never seen anything like
Keith's closet.
In it
there are trucks, and garages, and tents,
and cranes, and forts, and bikes, and puppets,
and games, and models, and superhero suits,
and hats and
he never plays with any of it.

They keep buying him all this stuff
and he never plays with it.
Day after day after day
it all sits in Keith's closet.

You ought to go over his place sometime
and have a look.
Keith's closet.
Wow!

Two Cats

When we opened the door late
to see what had happened to the sky
there were two cats
crouching among the snowdunes
pretending they were fireside laps.
The beads in their eyes stole some of
our kitchen light
and spilt it onto the path.
So we put down the bones of a chop there too
saying: there's some marrow inside that, you know —
but they didn't believe it was for them
and sat still thawing their patches
like two warm loaves
and groaning that we hadn't put it near enough
seeing that they had put their feet to bed by now.

Eddie in Bed (Eddie, my second son)

Sometimes I look real tired,
because you see
when most people are fast asleep
and I'm fast asleep
I hear,
"waaaaaaaaaaaaaaaaaaaaaaaaa."
That's the baby, Eddie.
So I get out of bed
and he's sitting up in bed
and he has these nightmares.
Not nightmares like you have,
like Dracula biting your head off or something.
He has nightmares about people taking his dinner
        away from him.
So one night I go in there
and he's sitting up in bed
lifting his arms above his head
and banging them down
screaming,
"I want my cookies I want my cookies."

Now if you can imagine that,
you can also imagine
that at this time he was sleeping
in the same bed as his brother, Joe.
Who was six.

And you have to imagine his brother's head
is right next to Eddie's hip.
Think about it.
Eddies hands go above his head and
Wham
down by his side
right on Joe's head.
"I want my cookies I want my cookies."
So Joe lifts his head and goes,
"What's going on?"
Wham
"I want my cookies."
"What's going on?"
Wham
"I want my cookies,"
"What's going on?"
Wham
"I want my cookies."

"Stop it, Eddie" — wham back
"I want my cookies."
Wham.
"Okay, fellas," I say,
"Cut it out."
And I lift Eddie up and I take him into our bed.

What a stupid thing to do.

You see
most people sleep with their head
on the pillow

and their feet at the other end of the bed.
When Eddie comes into our bed
he sleeps with his head next to my wife's head
and his feet in my ear.

And you have to imagine those feet
sticking in my ear.
And the toes.
Those toes are going
wiggly wiggly wiggly
down my ear.
All night.
So by the time I get up
in the morning
I'm very tired
and very cross.

But I can always get even with him
in the morning
'cause he hates having his diaper changed . . .

Moonshot

```
        5
        4
        3
        2
        1 rocket
        2 the moon
        3 flew it
what 4?
```

Ice Cream

At home,
when we had ice cream
we'd all sit around eating it
going
"Mmmm, this is nice. This is really nice."
But then my dad'd say,
"You know what this could use?
Just a little bit of fruit salad with it."

So next time we had ice cream
we had ice cream
and
a little bit of fruit salad with it,
and we'd all sit around eating it
going,
"Mmmm, this is nice, this is really nice."
But then my dad'd say,
"You know what this could use?
Just a few chopped nuts on the top.
That would really make this perfect."

So next time we had ice cream
we had ice cream, a little bit of fruit salad
and
a few chopped nuts over the top,

and we'd all be sitting around eating it
going
"Mmmmm, this is nice, this is really nice."
But then my dad'd say,
"You know what this could use?
A few of those
little tiny bits of chocolate
scattered over the top
that would make it — "

But my mom wouldn't let him say any more.
She goes,
"You're always the same, you are.
Nothing's good enough for you, is it?
I'll tell you something —
if you don't like this café
find another one.
You know why you're like this?
I'll tell you.
It was your *bubbe*.*
She pampered you.
You were pampered, you were.
All I ever hear is,
'No one ever makes it like my *bubbe* did.'
Well, you can get this into your head:
I'M NOT YOUR *BUBBE*."

And my dad'd turn to us and go
"What did I say?
What did I say wrong?
All I said was,

'A few little bits of chocolate
scattered over the top
would be very nice.'
What's wrong with saying that?
A few bits of chocolate
would be very nice, wouldn't they?
What's all the fuss about?
What
is
all
the
fuss
about?"

* *bubbe* = grandmother

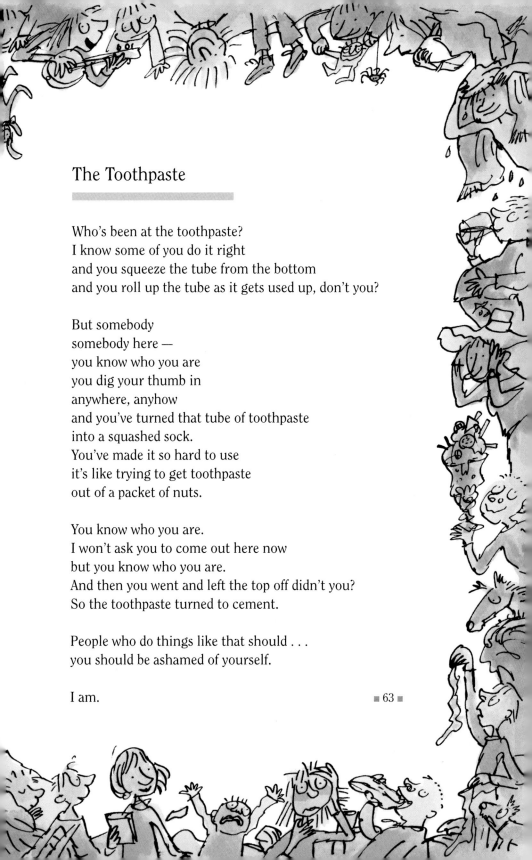

The Toothpaste

Who's been at the toothpaste?
I know some of you do it right
and you squeeze the tube from the bottom
and you roll up the tube as it gets used up, don't you?

But somebody
somebody here —
you know who you are
you dig your thumb in
anywhere, anyhow
and you've turned that tube of toothpaste
into a squashed sock.
You've made it so hard to use
it's like trying to get toothpaste
out of a packet of nuts.

You know who you are.
I won't ask you to come out here now
but you know who you are.
And then you went and left the top off didn't you?
So the toothpaste turned to cement.

People who do things like that should . . .
you should be ashamed of yourself.

I am.

The Man

The man on the corner
with broken glasses
sits on the bench
and watches who passes.

Thirty-Two Laps

One Tuesday when I was about
ten
I swam thirty-two laps
which is one mile.
And when I climbed out of the
water
I felt like a big, fat lump of jelly
and my legs were like rubber
and there was this huge man
there
with tremendous muscles all
over him
and I went up to him and said
"I've just swum a mile."
And he said,
"How many laps was that
then?"
"Thirty-two," I said.
And the man said,
"I've got a lad here who can
do ninety."

Hot Food

We sit down to eat
and the potato's a bit hot
so I only put a little bit on my fork
and I blow
whooph whooph
until it's cool
just cool
then into the mouth
nice.
And there's my brother
he's doing the same
whooph whooph
into the mouth
nice.
There's my mom
she's doing the same
whooph whooph
into the mouth
nice.
But my dad.
My dad.
What does he do?
He stuffs a great big chunk of potato
into his mouth.

Then
that really does it.
His eyes pop out
he flaps his hands
he blows, he puffs, he yells
he bobs his head up and down
he spits bits of potato
all over his plate
and he turns to us and he says,
"Watch out everybody —
the potato's real hot."

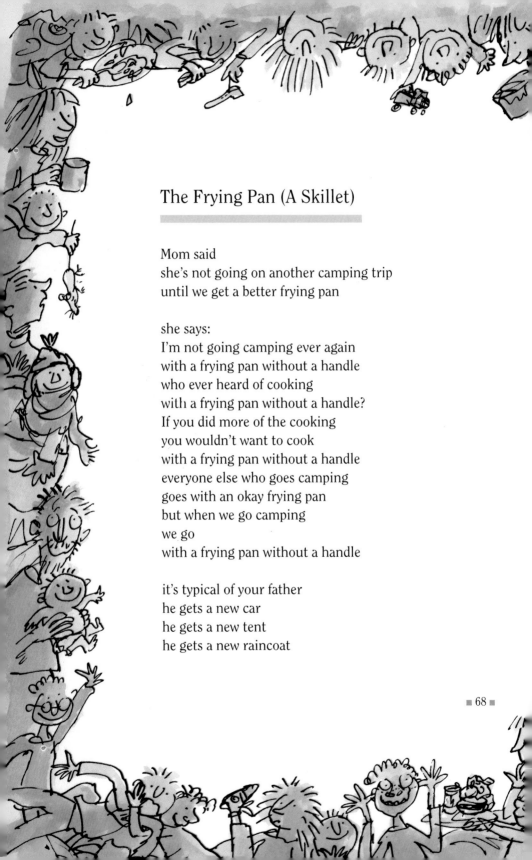

The Frying Pan (A Skillet)

Mom said
she's not going on another camping trip
until we get a better frying pan

she says:
I'm not going camping ever again
with a frying pan without a handle
who ever heard of cooking
with a frying pan without a handle?
If you did more of the cooking
you wouldn't want to cook
with a frying pan without a handle
everyone else who goes camping
goes with an okay frying pan
but when we go camping
we go
with a frying pan without a handle

it's typical of your father
he gets a new car
he gets a new tent
he gets a new raincoat

but I'm cooking
with a frying pan without a handle
I've sat there for hours and hours
trying to fry onions
trying to fry liver
trying to fry bacon and eggs
and I'm trying to do it all
with a frying pan without a handle

there are good frying pans these days
nice ones
I've seen them
people go camping with them
not rich people
people like us
they sit there every night
with their nice frying pans
having a nice time
but what have we got?

A frying pan without a handle.

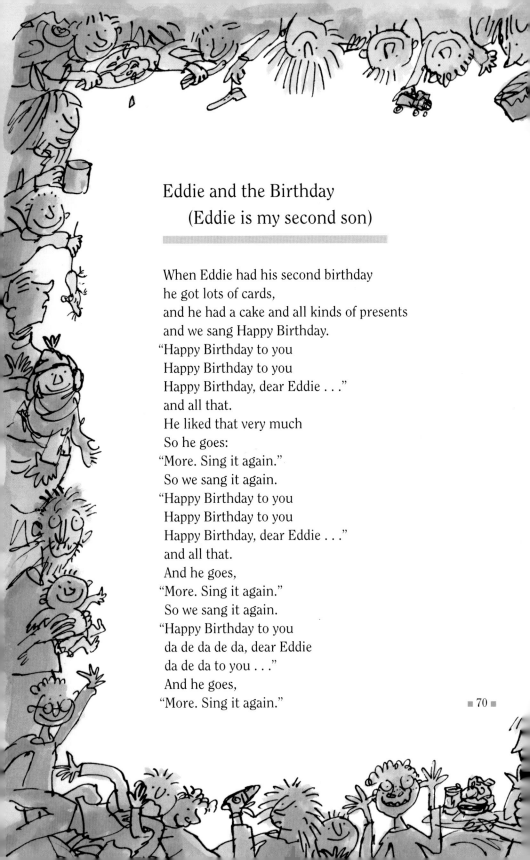

Eddie and the Birthday
(Eddie is my second son)

When Eddie had his second birthday
he got lots of cards,
and he had a cake and all kinds of presents
and we sang Happy Birthday.
"Happy Birthday to you
Happy Birthday to you
Happy Birthday, dear Eddie . . ."
and all that.
He liked that very much
So he goes:
"More. Sing it again."
So we sang it again.
"Happy Birthday to you
Happy Birthday to you
Happy Birthday, dear Eddie . . ."
and all that.
And he goes,
"More. Sing it again."
So we sang it again.
"Happy Birthday to you
da de da de da, dear Eddie
da de da to you . . ."
And he goes,
"More. Sing it again."

■ 70 ■

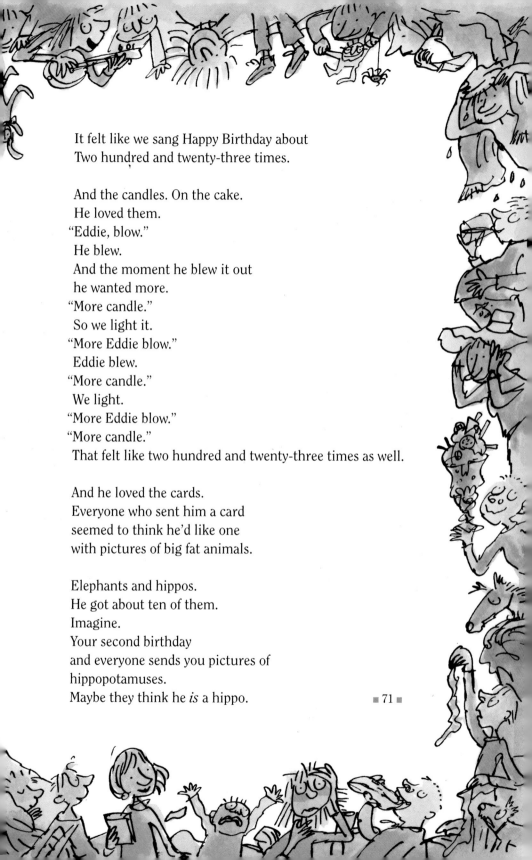

It felt like we sang Happy Birthday about
Two hundred and twenty-three times.

And the candles. On the cake.
He loved them.
"Eddie, blow."
He blew.
And the moment he blew it out
he wanted more.
"More candle."
So we light it.
"More Eddie blow."
Eddie blew.
"More candle."
We light.
"More Eddie blow."
"More candle."
That felt like two hundred and twenty-three times as well.

And he loved the cards.
Everyone who sent him a card
seemed to think he'd like one
with pictures of big fat animals.

Elephants and hippos.
He got about ten of them.
Imagine.
Your second birthday
and everyone sends you pictures of
hippopotamuses.
Maybe they think he *is* a hippo.

Anyway he had a nice birthday.
Next day he gets up
comes downstairs
and he looks around
and he goes,
"More happy birfdy."
So I go,
"That was yesterday, Eddie."
"More happy birfdy."
"But it isn't your birfdy — I mean birthday . . . "
"More happy birfdy."

Now, you don't cross Eddie.
He throws tantrums.
We call them wobblies.
"Look out, he's going to throw a wobbly!"
And the face starts going red,
the arms start going up and down,
the screaming starts winding up
he starts jumping up and down
and there he is —
throwing a wobbly.

So I thought,
"We don't want to have a wobbly over this one."
So we started singing Happy Birthday all over again.
Two hundred and twenty-three times.
Then he says
"More candles."

"We haven't got any," we say
  (Lies, of course, we had).
"More candles . . ."
  So out came the candles
  and yes —
"Eddie blow."
  He blew.
"More candle."
  And off we go again —
  Two hundred and twenty-three times.

And then he says,
"Letters, More."
  Well, of course no one sent him any more,
  so while I'm singing more happy birfdys,
  my wife was stuffing all the cards
  into envelopes and sticking them down.
  So we hand over all his cards again
  and out came all the hippopotamuses again.

So he's very pleased.
And that's how Eddie had two birthdays.
Lucky for us
he'd forgotten by the third day.

Maybe he thinks when you're two you have two birthdays
and when you're three you have three birthdays
and when you're seventy-eight you . . .

Sneakers

See me in my sneakers
speeding around the house
see me in my sneakers
speeding down the street
see me in my sneakers
speeding to the stores.

See me in my sneakers
kicking a tennis ball

see me in my sneakers
kicking a hard brick wall

see me in my sneakers
kicking my friend's leg.

See me in my sneakers
there's a hole in my toe
see me in my sneakers
the sole's worn through

you can't see me in my sneakers
they're in the trash can.

See my sneakers!

Say Please

I'll have a please sandwich cheese
No I mean a knees sandwich please
Sorry I mean a fleas sandwich please
No a please sandwich please
No   no — it's okay
I'll have a donut.

Going through the Old Photos

Me, my dad
and my brother
we were looking through the old photos.
Pictures of my dad with a broken leg
and my mom with big flappy shorts on
and me on a tricycle
when we got to one of my mom
with a baby on her knee, and I go,
"Is that me or Brian?"
And my dad says,
"Let's have a look.
It isn't you or Brian," he says.
"It's Alan.
He died.
He would have been
two years younger than Brian
and two years older than you.
He was a lovely baby."

"How did he die?"
"Whooping cough.
I was away at the time.
He coughed himself to death in Connie's arms.
The terrible thing is,
it wouldn't happen today,
but it was during the war, you see,
and they didn't have much medicine.

■ 76 ■

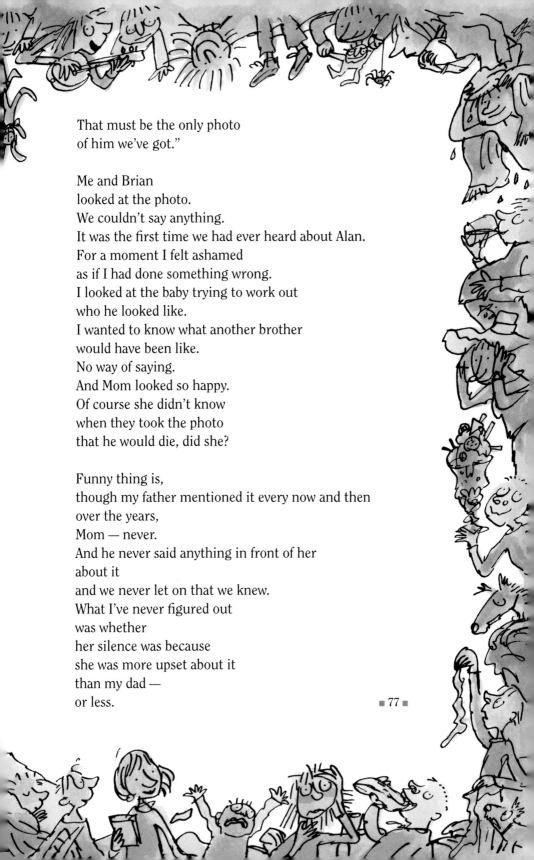

That must be the only photo
of him we've got."

Me and Brian
looked at the photo.
We couldn't say anything.
It was the first time we had ever heard about Alan.
For a moment I felt ashamed
as if I had done something wrong.
I looked at the baby trying to work out
who he looked like.
I wanted to know what another brother
would have been like.
No way of saying.
And Mom looked so happy.
Of course she didn't know
when they took the photo
that he would die, did she?

Funny thing is,
though my father mentioned it every now and then
over the years,
Mom — never.
And he never said anything in front of her
about it
and we never let on that we knew.
What I've never figured out
was whether
her silence was because
she was more upset about it
than my dad —
or less.

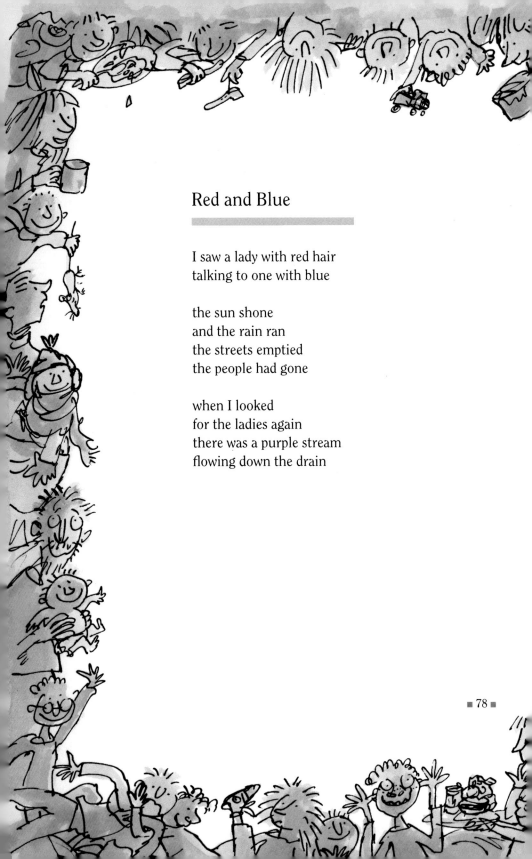

Red and Blue

I saw a lady with red hair
talking to one with blue

the sun shone
and the rain ran
the streets emptied
the people had gone

when I looked
for the ladies again
there was a purple stream
flowing down the drain

Cold Fly

From the winter wind
a cold fly
came to our window
where we had frozen our noses
and warmed his feet on the glass

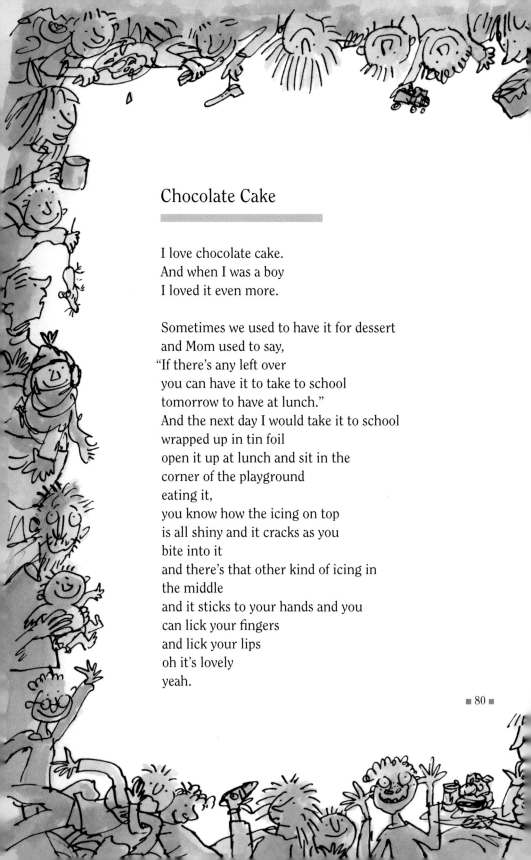

Chocolate Cake

I love chocolate cake.
And when I was a boy
I loved it even more.

Sometimes we used to have it for dessert
and Mom used to say,
"If there's any left over
you can have it to take to school
tomorrow to have at lunch."
And the next day I would take it to school
wrapped up in tin foil
open it up at lunch and sit in the
corner of the playground
eating it,
you know how the icing on top
is all shiny and it cracks as you
bite into it
and there's that other kind of icing in
the middle
and it sticks to your hands and you
can lick your fingers
and lick your lips
oh it's lovely
yeah.

Anyway,
once we had this chocolate cake for dessert
and later I went to bed
but while I was in bed
I found myself waking up
licking my lips
and smiling.
I woke up completely.
"The chocolate cake."
It was the first thing
I thought of.
I could almost see it
so I thought,
what if I go downstairs
and have a little nibble, yeah?
It was all dark
everyone was in bed
so it must have been really late
but I got out of bed,
crept out of the door

there's always a creaky floorboard, isn't there?

Past Mom and Dad's room,

careful not to step on bits of broken toys
or bits of Lego
you know what it's like stepping on Lego
with your bare feet,

yowwww
shhhhhhh

downstairs
into the kitchen
open the fridge
and there it is
all shining.

So I take it out of the fridge
put it on the table
and I see that
there's a few crumbs lying about on the plate,
so I lick my finger and run my finger all over the crumbs
scooping them up
and put them into my mouth

ooooooooommmmmmmmm

nice.

Then
I look again
and on one side where it's been cut,
it's all crumbly.
So I take a knife
I think I'll just tidy that up a bit,

cut off the crumbly bits
scoop them all up
and into the mouth

ooooooommm   mmmm
nice.

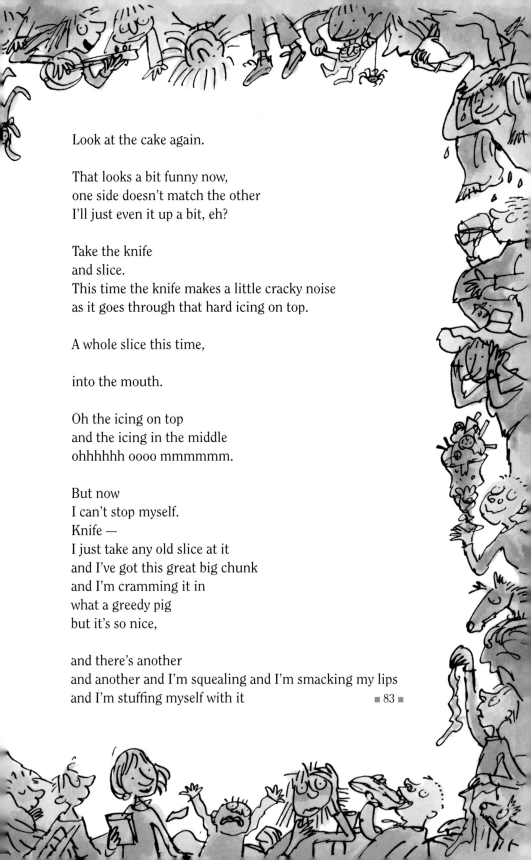

Look at the cake again.

That looks a bit funny now,
one side doesn't match the other
I'll just even it up a bit, eh?

Take the knife
and slice.
This time the knife makes a little cracky noise
as it goes through that hard icing on top.

A whole slice this time,

into the mouth.

Oh the icing on top
and the icing in the middle
ohhhhhh oooo mmmmmm.

But now
I can't stop myself.
Knife —
I just take any old slice at it
and I've got this great big chunk
and I'm cramming it in
what a greedy pig
but it's so nice,

and there's another
and another and I'm squealing and I'm smacking my lips
and I'm stuffing myself with it   ■ 83 ■

and
before I know
I've eaten all of it.
The whole cake.
I look at the plate.
It's all gone.

Oh no
they're bound to notice, aren't they,
a whole chocolate cake doesn't just disappear
does it?

What shall I do?

I know. I'll wash the plate,
and the knife

and put them away and maybe no one
will notice, eh?

So I do that
and creep creep creep
back to bed
into bed
doze off
licking my lips
with a lovely feeling in my belly.
Mmmmmmmmm.

In the morning I get up,
go downstairs,

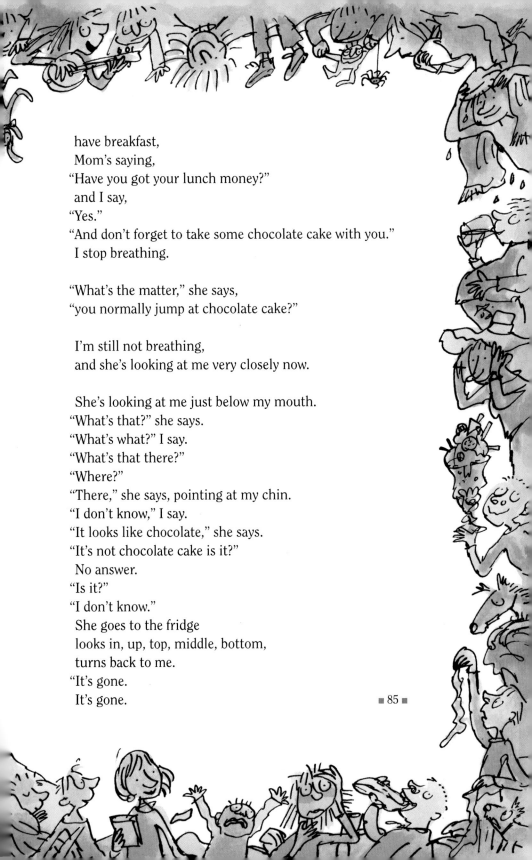

have breakfast,
Mom's saying,
"Have you got your lunch money?"
and I say,
"Yes."
"And don't forget to take some chocolate cake with you."
I stop breathing.

"What's the matter," she says,
"you normally jump at chocolate cake?"

I'm still not breathing,
and she's looking at me very closely now.

She's looking at me just below my mouth.
"What's that?" she says.
"What's what?" I say.
"What's that there?"
"Where?"
"There," she says, pointing at my chin.
"I don't know," I say.
"It looks like chocolate," she says.
"It's not chocolate cake is it?"
No answer.
"Is it?"
"I don't know."
She goes to the fridge
looks in, up, top, middle, bottom,
turns back to me.
"It's gone.
It's gone.

■ 85 ■

You haven't eaten it, have you?"
"I don't know."
"You don't know? You don't know if you've eaten a whole
chocolate cake or not?
When? When did you eat it?"

So I told her,

and she said
well what could she say?
"That's the last time I give you any cake to take
to school.
Now go. Get out
no wait
not before you've washed your dirty sticky face."
I went upstairs
looked in the mirror
and there it was,
just below my mouth,
a chocolate blob.
The give-away.
Maybe she'll forget about it by next week.

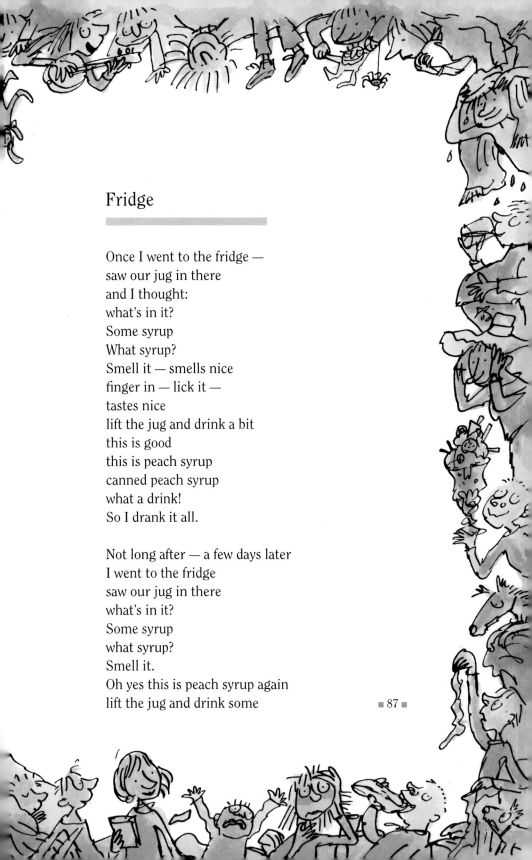

Fridge

Once I went to the fridge —
saw our jug in there
and I thought:
what's in it?
Some syrup
What syrup?
Smell it — smells nice
finger in — lick it —
tastes nice
lift the jug and drink a bit
this is good
this is peach syrup
canned peach syrup
what a drink!
So I drank it all.

Not long after — a few days later
I went to the fridge
saw our jug in there
what's in it?
Some syrup
what syrup?
Smell it.
Oh yes this is peach syrup again
lift the jug and drink some

drink some more, drink some more
drink it all.

Not long after — a few days later
I went to the fridge
saw our jug in there
what's in it?
Some syrup — yes!
Here we go again
lift the jug and fill my mouth
with that thick sweet juice . . .

Uckg!

This isn't peach
this is uckg
my mouth is full of oil
thick cooking oil

I wonder who put that there . . .

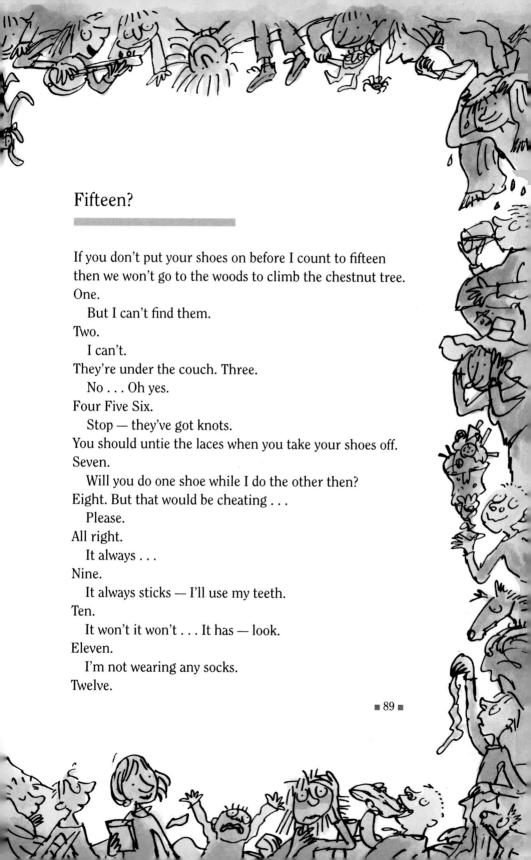

Fifteen?

If you don't put your shoes on before I count to fifteen
then we won't go to the woods to climb the chestnut tree.
One.
    But I can't find them.
Two.
    I can't.
They're under the couch. Three.
    No . . . Oh yes.
Four Five Six.
    Stop — they've got knots.
You should untie the laces when you take your shoes off.
Seven.
    Will you do one shoe while I do the other then?
Eight. But that would be cheating . . .
    Please.
All right.
    It always . . .
Nine.
    It always sticks — I'll use my teeth.
Ten.
    It won't it won't . . . It has — look.
Eleven.
    I'm not wearing any socks.
Twelve.

Stop counting stop counting. (Mom where are my socks Mom?)
THEY'RE IN YOUR SHOES. WHERE YOU LEFT THEM.
   I didn't.
Thirteen.
   Oh they're inside out and upside down and bundled up.
Fourteen.
   Have you done the knot on the shoe you were . . .
Yes. Put it on the right foot.
   But socks don't have a right and wrong foot.
The shoes, silly . . . Fourteen and a half.
   I am I am. Wait.
   Don't go to the woods without me.
   Look that's one shoe already.
Fourteen and three quarters.
   There!
You haven't tied the bows yet.
   We could do them on the way there?
No we won't. Fourteen and seven eighths.
   Help me then —
   You know I'm not fast at bows.
Fourteen and fifteen sixteenths.
   A single bow is all right, isn't it?
Fifteen. We're off.
   See I did it.

   Didn't I?

After Dark

Outside after dark
trains hum and traffic lights wink
after dark, after dark.

In here after dark
curtains shake and closets creak
after dark, after dark.

Under the covers after dark
I twiddle my toes and hug my pillow
after dark, after dark.

Peas

Peas for breakfast please he said
and a plateful of peas is what he got

and when he went to bed last night
I heard him say: more peas please.

You know, I don't think he eats much else
one full bowl three times a day.

It would fill a room all those peas you know
but I think
even if he had to wade up to his knees in peas
he would still come here saying: more peas please.

Don't Tell Your Mother

When my mom went to night school
my dad would say,
"Don't tell your mother — let's have *matzo bray* *
she always says:
'Don't give the boys that greasy stuff.
It's bad for them.'
So don't tell her, okay?"

So he broke up the *matzos*
put them into water to soften them up.
Then he fried them
till they were glazed and crisp.
"It tastes best fried in *hinner shmaltz,***
skimmed off chicken soup," he says,
"but olive oil will do."
Then he beat three eggs
and poured it on over the frying matzos
till it was all cooked.

It tasted yummy.
We loved it.
Then we washed everything up,
absolutely everything
and we went to bed.

Next day,
Mom says to us,
"What did your father cook you last night?"

Silence.

"What did your father cook you last night?"

Oh, you know . . . stuff . . .
. . . egg on toast, I think.

* *matzo bray* = the Yiddish name of a dish made of *matzos* and egg. Matzos is the word for unleavened bread and tastes like water biscuits.
** *hinner shmaltz* = the Yiddish word for chicken fat.

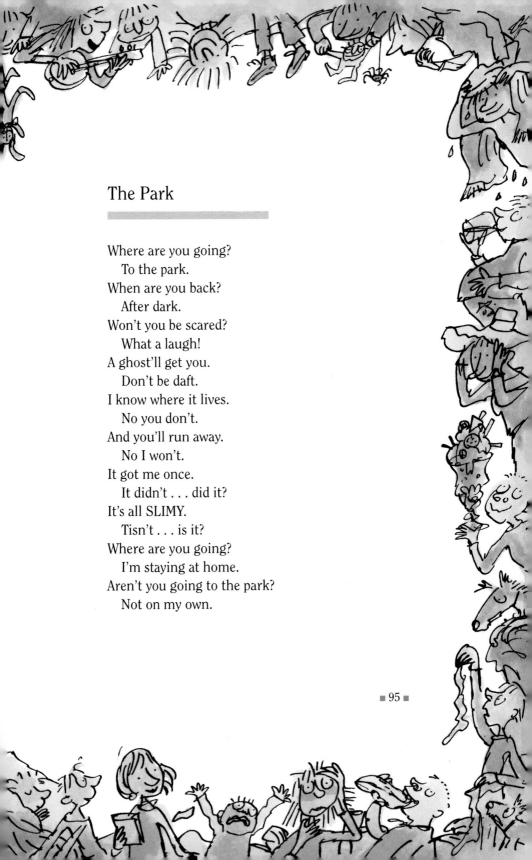

The Park

Where are you going?
   To the park.
When are you back?
   After dark.
Won't you be scared?
   What a laugh!
A ghost'll get you.
   Don't be daft.
I know where it lives.
   No you don't.
And you'll run away.
   No I won't.
It got me once.
   It didn't . . . did it?
It's all SLIMY.
   Tisn't . . . is it?
Where are you going?
   I'm staying at home.
Aren't you going to the park?
   Not on my own.

Don't

Don't do,
Don't do,
Don't do that.
Don't pull faces,
Don't tease the cat.

Don't pick your ears,
Don't be rude at school.
Who do they think I am?

Some kind of fool?

One day
they'll say
Don't put toffee in my coffee
don't pour gravy on the baby
don't put beer in his ear
don't stick your toes up his nose.

Don't put confetti on the spaghetti
and don't squash peas on your knees.

Don't put ants in your pants
don't put mustard in the custard

don't chuck jelly at the telly

and don't throw fruit at a computer
don't throw fruit at a computer.

Don't what?
Don't throw fruit at a computer.
Don't what?
Don't throw fruit at a computer.
Who do they think I am?
Some kind of fool?

Angry Hens

The angry hens from Never-when
had a fight and lost their legs.
Now it's hot
where they squat
and they're laying soft-boiled eggs.

No One In

Sometimes you come home
and there's no one in.
There are no lights on
no food ready
no t.v.
no one laughing
no jokes
just you
on your own.

That's when my brain
starts doing things:
you know,
murders and mad dogs stuff.

I'll tell you what I do.
When I open the door
I shove it really hard and fast
and it bangs against the wall
real loud

so if he's hiding behind the door
he'll get it right on the nose.

I never have got him
I'll tell you what did happen, though.
The door handle
made a great big hole in the wall.

Danny

Your brother Danny's got a golden nose
and fish swim out of his eyes
Your brother Danny's got legs like rhubarb
and ears like apple pies.

Dogs

Down behind the trash can
I met a dog called Sid.
He could smell a bone inside
but couldn't lift the lid.

Down behind the trash can
I met a dog called Jim.
He didn't know me
and I didn't know him.

Down behind the trash can
I met a dog called Sid.
He said he didn't know me,
but I'm pretty sure he did.

Down behind the trash can
I met a dog called Jack.
"Are you going anywhere?" I said.
"No. I'm just coming back."

Down behind the trash can
I met a dog called Billy.
"I'm not talking to you," I said,
"if you're going to be silly."

Down behind the trash can
I met a dog called Barry.
He tried to take the can away
but it was too heavy to carry.

Down behind the trash can
I met a dog called Mary.
"I wish I wasn't a dog," she said,
"I wish I was a canary."

Down behind the trash can
I met a dog called Ted.
"Leave me alone," he says,
"I'm just going to bed."

Down behind the trash can
I met a dog called Felicity.
"It's a bit dark here," she said,
"They've cut off the electricity."

Down behind the trash can
I met a dog called Roger.
"Do you own this bin?" I said.
"No. I'm only the lodger."

Down behind the trash can
I met a dog called Sue.
"What are you doing here?" I said.
"I've got nothing else to do."

Down behind the trash can
I met a dog called Anne.
"I'm just off now," she said,
"to see a dog about a man."

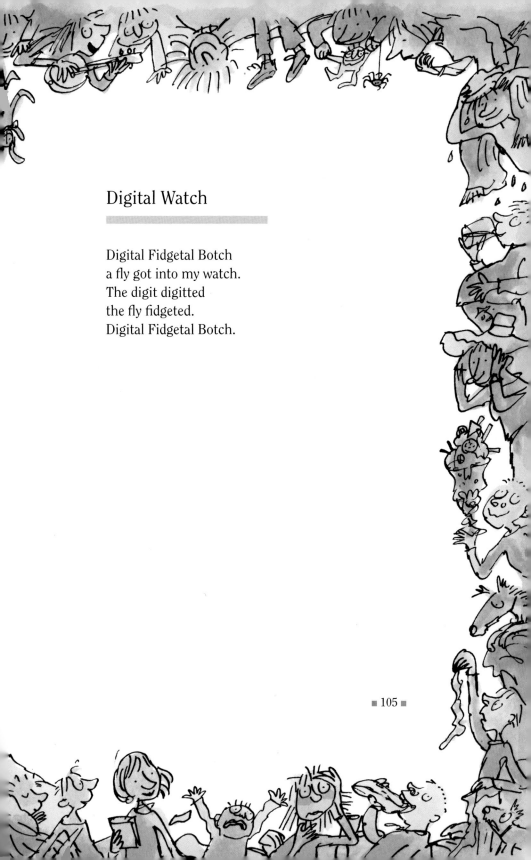

Digital Watch

Digital Fidgetal Botch
a fly got into my watch.
The digit digitted
the fly fidgeted.
Digital Fidgetal Botch.

The Car Trip

Mom says:
"All right, you two,
    this is a very long car trip.
I want you two to be good.
I'm driving and I can't drive properly
    if you two are going crazy in the back.
Do you understand?"

So we say,
"Okay, Mom, okay. Don't worry."
And off we go.

And we start The Moaning:
Can I have a drink?
I want some chips.
Can I open my window?
He's got my book.
Get off me.
Ow, that's my ear!

And Mom tries to be exciting:
"Look out the window
    There's a lamp post."

And we go on with The Moaning:
Can I have some candy?

He's sitting on me.
Are we there yet?
Don't scratch.
You never yell at him.
Now he's biting his nails.
I want a drink. I want a drink.

And Mom tries to be exciting again:
"Look out the window
There's a tree."

And we go on:
My hands are sticky.
He's playing with the door handle now.
I feel sick.
Your nose is all runny.
Don't pull my hair.
He's punching me, Mom.
That's really dangerous, you know.
Mom, he's spitting.

And Mom says:
"All right I'm stopping the car.
I AM STOPPING THE CAR."

She stops the car.

"Now, if you two don't stop it
I'm going to put you out of the car
and leave you by the side of the road."

He started it.
Did not. He did.

"I don't care who started it
I can't drive properly
if you two go crazy in the back.
Do you understand?"

And we say:
Okay, Mom, okay, don't worry.

Can I have a drink?

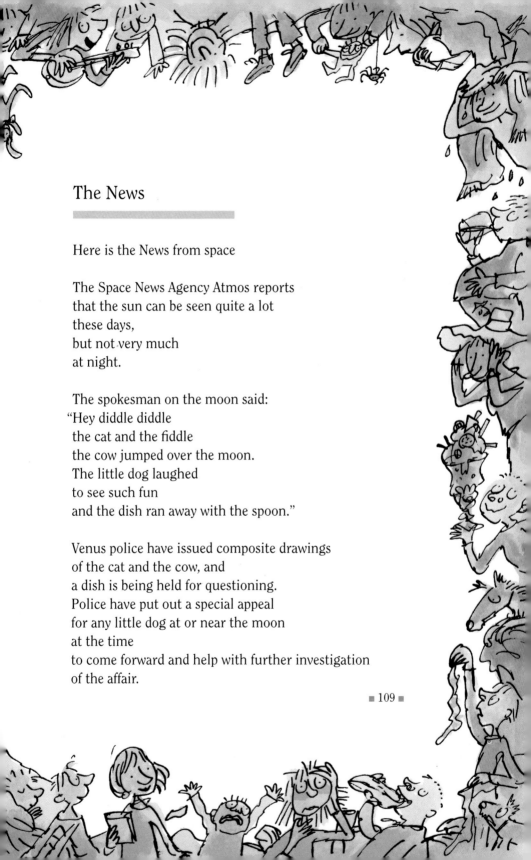

The News

Here is the News from space

The Space News Agency Atmos reports
that the sun can be seen quite a lot
these days,
but not very much
at night.

The spokesman on the moon said:
"Hey diddle diddle
the cat and the fiddle
the cow jumped over the moon.
The little dog laughed
to see such fun
and the dish ran away with the spoon."

Venus police have issued composite drawings
of the cat and the cow, and
a dish is being held for questioning.
Police have put out a special appeal
for any little dog at or near the moon
at the time
to come forward and help with further investigation
of the affair.

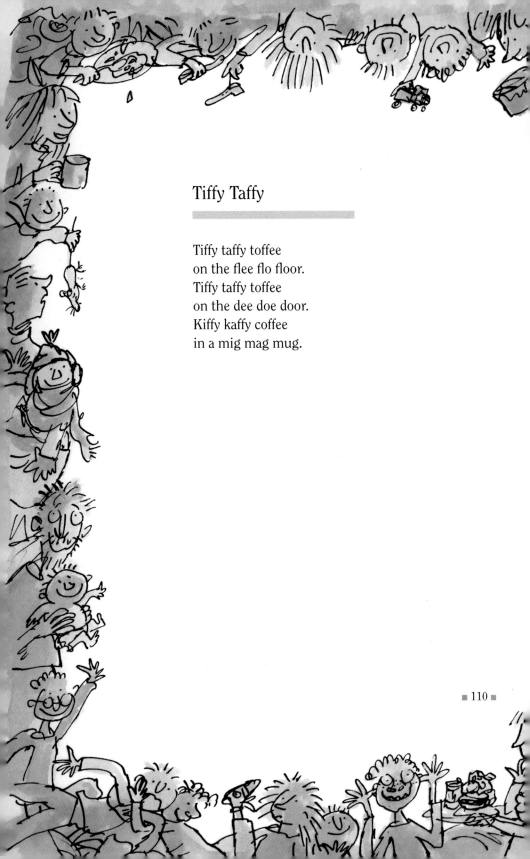

Tiffy Taffy

Tiffy taffy toffee
on the flee flo floor.
Tiffy taffy toffee
on the dee doe door.
Kiffy kaffy coffee
in a mig mag mug.

Bubah and Zaida
(Visiting Mom's Mom and Dad)

We sometimes see them on Sunday.
They live in a dark room at the end of a dark corridor
and Bubah kisses us all when we arrive.
She looks like Mom but very silver and bent at the
    middle,
which we will all look like one day says Mom's father.
Dad always looks fed up because he doesn't want to come
but Mom talks to them properly.
Zaida looks tired
and pretends that the quarter he's going to give me
disappears into the ceiling along with my nose
if I'm not careful — snap — and there's his thumb in his
    fist,
and he beats me at checkers, dominoes, chutes-and-
    ladders,
and even dice
and he's got a bottle with a boat in it
and we go for walks on Hackney Downs
which he calls Acknee Dans.
And all the old men there say, "Hallo, Frank,"
and while we're walking along he says:
"What's to become of us, Mickie, what's to become of us?"
and I don't know what to answer.

And he shows me to Uncle Hymie
who looked out of his window and said:
"Is that big boy your grandson, Frank?" (even though he
        knows my name)
because that's the way they talk.
And when we get back we eat chopped herring or
        chopped liver
which is my favorite
and Bubah tells stories that go on for hours
about people she knows who are ill or people who've
had to pay too much money and at the end of the story
it always seems as if she's been cheated.
And once she took a whole afternoon to tell Mom
how to make pickled cucumber and she kept saying:
"Just add a little salt to taste, a little salt to taste,
just taste it and see if there's enough salt,
to make sure if there's enough salt — just taste and see."
And she calls me, 'Tattele' which means 'Little Daddy' and
        rubs my hair and bites her lips
as though I'm going to run away
and so she shakes her head and
says, "Oy yoy yoy yoy yoy."
But Zaida goes to sleep in the old brown armchair
with his hands on the pockets of his flappy blue pants
and when we go Mom frowns
and Zaida holds my hand in his puffy old hand,
keeps ducking his head in little jerks
and says to us all, come again soon,
but I'd be afraid to go all the way on my own
and it's very dark and the bathroom is outside

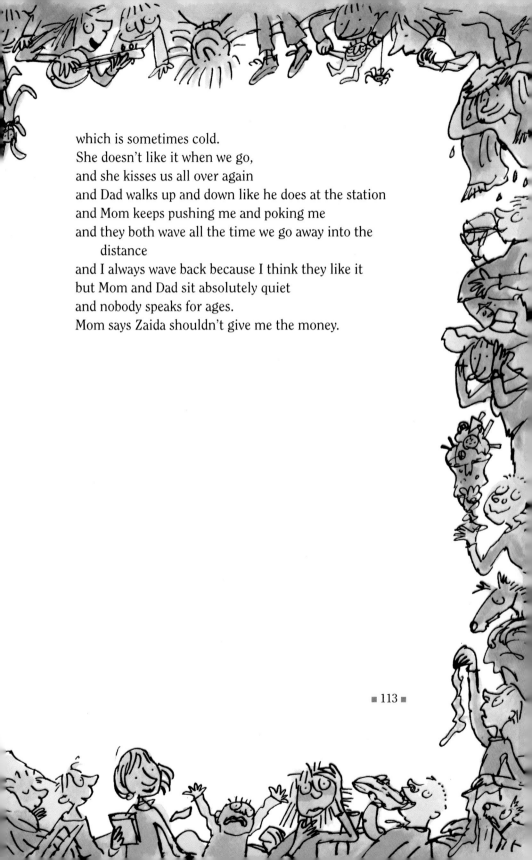

which is sometimes cold.
She doesn't like it when we go,
and she kisses us all over again
and Dad walks up and down like he does at the station
and Mom keeps pushing me and poking me
and they both wave all the time we go away into the
    distance
and I always wave back because I think they like it
but Mom and Dad sit absolutely quiet
and nobody speaks for ages.
Mom says Zaida shouldn't give me the money.

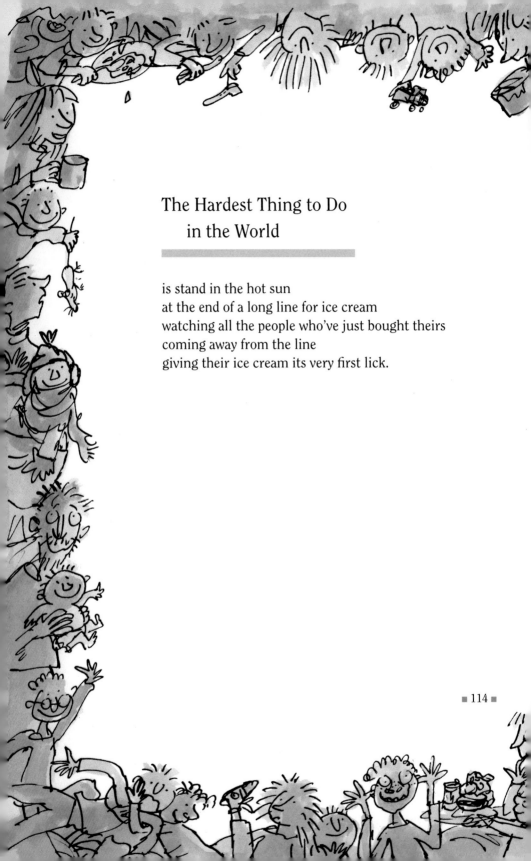

The Hardest Thing to Do
in the World

is stand in the hot sun
at the end of a long line for ice cream
watching all the people who've just bought theirs
coming away from the line
giving their ice cream its very first lick.

Newcomers

My father came here
from another country.
My father's mother came here
from another country
but my father's father
stayed behind.

So my dad had no dad here
and I never saw him at all.

One day in spring
some things arrived:
a few old papers,
a few old photos
and — oh yes —
a hulky bulky thick checked jacket
that belonged to the man
I would have called "Granddad."
The Man Who Stayed Behind.

But I kept that jacket
and I wore it
and I wore it
and I wore it
till it wore right through
at the back.

The Hidebehind

Have you seen the Hidebehind?
I don't think you will, mind you,
because as you're running through the dark
the Hidebehind's behind you.

Mm? (Joe is my first son)

I say:
What are you doing? And our little boy Joe says,
Mm?
What d'you think you're doing?
Mm?
Why did you do that?
Mm?
The peanut butter. All over your blanket.
Mm?
And the talcum powder?
Mm?
Don't do it — do you understand?
Mm?
Or there'll be trouble. And Joe says,
Trouble,
and runs off laughing.

Late

Late last night
I lay in bed
driving buses
in my head.

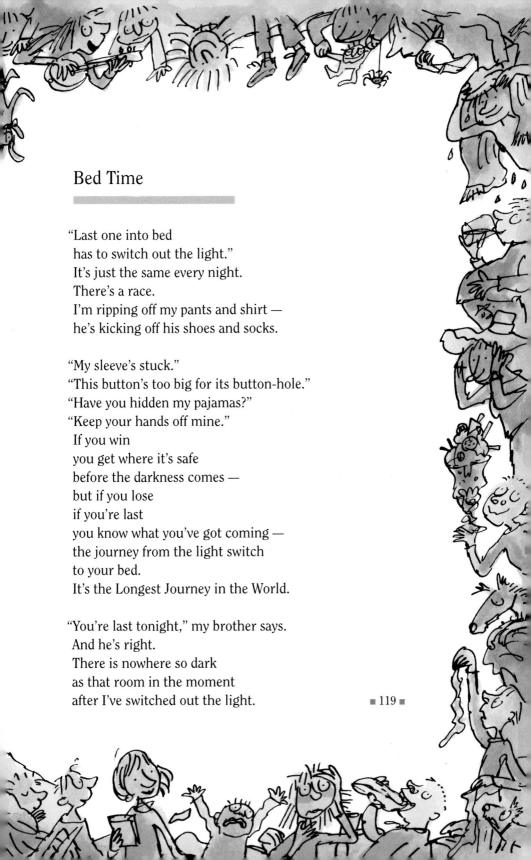

Bed Time

"Last one into bed
 has to switch out the light."
It's just the same every night.
There's a race.
I'm ripping off my pants and shirt —
 he's kicking off his shoes and socks.

"My sleeve's stuck."
"This button's too big for its button-hole."
"Have you hidden my pajamas?"
"Keep your hands off mine."
 If you win
 you get where it's safe
 before the darkness comes —
 but if you lose
 if you're last
 you know what you've got coming —
 the journey from the light switch
 to your bed.
 It's the Longest Journey in the World.

"You're last tonight," my brother says.
 And he's right.
 There is nowhere so dark
 as that room in the moment
 after I've switched out the light.

There is nowhere so full of dangerous things —
things that love dark places —
things that breathe only when I breathe
and hold their breath when I hold mine.
So I have to say:
"I'm not scared."
That face, grinning in the pattern on the wall
isn't a face —
"I'm not scared."

That prickle on the back of my neck
is only the label on my pajama top —
"I'm not scared,"
That moaning-moaning is nothing
but water in a pipe —
"I'm not scared."

Everything's going to be just fine
as soon as I get into that bed of mine.
Such a terrible shame
it's always the same
it takes so long
it takes so long
it takes so long
to get there.

From the light switch
to my bed.
It's the Longest Journey in the World.

Michael Rosen

Michael Rosen was born in 1946, the son of educators Harold and Connie Rosen. He began writing when he was about sixteen under the influence, he says, of a combination of the poetry of D.H. Lawrence, e.e. cummings, Carl Sandburg, and Robert Browning. His first published work was a play, *Backbone* (Faber, 1969), which was performed in London's Royal Court Theatre while he was still an undergraduate at Wadham College, Oxford University. His first work for children was *Mind Your Own Business* (Andre Deutsch, 1974), a book of poetry that critics have regarded as a groundbreaking collection as it opened the door to a new wave of child-centered, humorous, bitter-sweet poetry for children in the United Kingdom.

Since then he has divided his time between his all-action performances in theaters and schools, lectures to teachers and librarians on the role of literature in education, broadcasting on radio and TV (he hosts his own radio shows on the BBC), writing, journalism, compiling anthologies of stories and poems, and helping raise a family. He has over a hundred books to his name — that includes his many adaptions of folk tales — and has won several prestigious prizes including Best Book of the Year Award for his collaboration with Helen Oxenbury for *We're Going On A Bear Hunt* (Walker and McElderry, 1989).

Described as the "poet laureate of British youth," he has a string of collections with such provocative titles as *Quick Let's Get Out of Here, Wouldn't You Like to Know, You Tell Me,* and *Don't Put Mustard in the Custard.* It has not been easy to find a good selection of his original poetry in the United States. With *The Best of Michael Rosen* (RDR Books) this is now remedied.

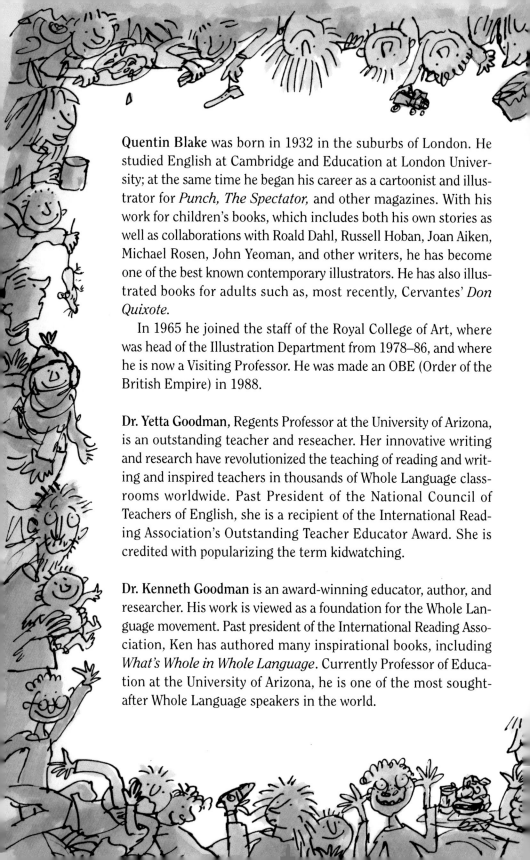

Quentin Blake was born in 1932 in the suburbs of London. He studied English at Cambridge and Education at London University; at the same time he began his career as a cartoonist and illustrator for *Punch, The Spectator,* and other magazines. With his work for children's books, which includes both his own stories as well as collaborations with Roald Dahl, Russell Hoban, Joan Aiken, Michael Rosen, John Yeoman, and other writers, he has become one of the best known contemporary illustrators. He has also illustrated books for adults such as, most recently, Cervantes' *Don Quixote.*

In 1965 he joined the staff of the Royal College of Art, where was head of the Illustration Department from 1978–86, and where he is now a Visiting Professor. He was made an OBE (Order of the British Empire) in 1988.

Dr. Yetta Goodman, Regents Professor at the University of Arizona, is an outstanding teacher and reseacher. Her innovative writing and research have revolutionized the teaching of reading and writing and inspired teachers in thousands of Whole Language classrooms worldwide. Past President of the National Council of Teachers of English, she is a recipient of the International Reading Association's Outstanding Teacher Educator Award. She is credited with popularizing the term kidwatching.

Dr. Kenneth Goodman is an award-winning educator, author, and researcher. His work is viewed as a foundation for the Whole Language movement. Past president of the International Reading Association, Ken has authored many inspirational books, including *What's Whole in Whole Language.* Currently Professor of Education at the University of Arizona, he is one of the most sought-after Whole Language speakers in the world.

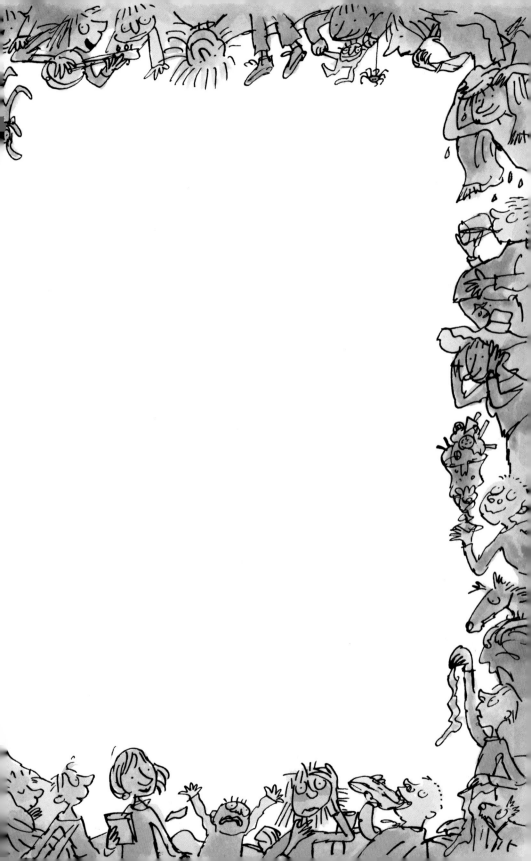

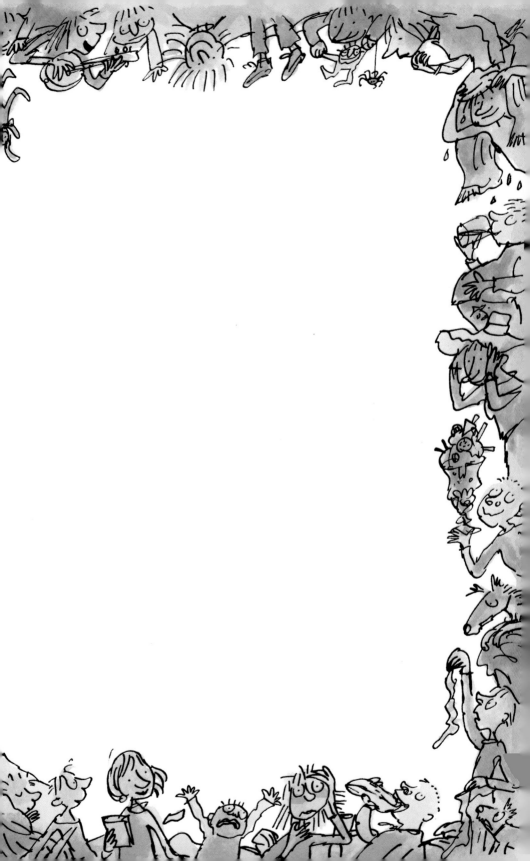